Klett Lektürehilfen

Clint Eastwood

Gran Torino

Interpretationshilfe für Oberstufe und Abitur

von
Johannes Wahl

Klett Lerntraining

Dr. Johannes Wahl, Gymnasiallehrer für Englisch, Deutsch und Geschichte in Baden-Württemberg

Die Lektürehilfe bezieht sich auf die DVD: Clint Eastwood: Gran Torino, Village Roadshow Pictures / Warner Brothers. 2008 Matten Productions GmbH & Co. KG. Die Zitate aus dem Film folgen den englischen Untertiteln der französischen Importversion.

Bildnachweis:
face to face Agentur GmbH, Hamburg: **55, 98, 101** (CapFSD/face to face); Film Still from „Gran Torino"; Clint Eastwood © 2008 Warner Brothers: **28**; PONS GmbH, Stuttgart: **24**

Bibliografische Information der Deutschen Nationalbibliothek
Die Deutsche Nationalbibliothek verzeichnet diese Publikation in der Deutschen Nationalbibliografie; detaillierte bibliografische Daten sind im Internet über http://dnb.dnb.de abrufbar

Das Werk und seine Teile sind urheberrechtlich geschützt. Jede Nutzung in anderen als den gesetzlich zugelassenen Fällen bedarf der vorherigen schriftlichen Einwilligung des Verlages. Hinweis zu § 52a UrhG: Weder das Werk noch seine Teile dürfen ohne eine solche Einwilligung eingescannt und in ein Netzwerk eingestellt werden. Dies gilt auch für Intranets von Schulen und sonstigen Bildungseinrichtungen. Fotomechanische Wiedergabe nur mit Genehmigung des Verlages.

1. Auflage 2017

© PONS GmbH, Stöckachstraße 11, 70190 Stuttgart 2017
Alle Rechte vorbehalten
www.klett-lerntraining.de
Teamleitung Sekundarstufe II: Christine Sämann
Umschlagfoto: face to face Agentur GmbH, Hamburg (CapFSD/face to face)
Satz: DOPPELPUNKT, Stuttgart
Druck: medienhaus Plump GmbH, Rheinbreitbach
Printed in Germany
ISBN: 978-3-12-923142-5

Contents

1 The Plot

Scene Index 5

Exposition 15

Gang Pressure on Thao 21

Hero to the Neighborhood 25

Painful Self-Recognition 29
Teaching Thao (How) to Become a Man 33
Escalating Violence 39
Walt's Death 42

2 Analysis and Interpretation

Narrative Structure 48

Setting 50

Characters 54

Walt Kowalski 54
Thao and the Hmong Community
   (Sue, Phong, Smokie and Spider) 61
Father Janovich 70

Themes 72

Racism in a Multicultural Society 72
(Gun) Violence 77
Concepts of Masculinity 80
Generation Gaps 85
Guilt and Redemption 90
The Ambiguity of Belonging 92

Symbols and Motifs 96

Cinematic Devices 100

Camera 100
Music and Lighting 104

3 Fast Facts

Outline 1: Structure 110
Outline 2: Setting 111
Outline 3: Walt Kowalski 112
Outline 4: Thao 113
Outline 5: Multicultural Society 114
Outline 6: The Ambiguity of Belonging 115
Outline 7: Symbols and Motifs 116
Outline 8: Cinematic Devices 117

4 Model Tasks and Answers

1. Walt and Thao 120
2. Walt and his Family 123
3. Portrayal of the Hmong Community 126
4. Ambiguous Identities 129
5. Guilt and Redemption 132
6. Language 134
7. *Gran Torino* – A Portrait of Contemporary America? ... 136
8. *Gran Torino* and Tom Franklin's Novel *Crooked Letter, Crooked Letter* 138

Bibliography 141
Index 143

① The Plot

Scene Index

Scene	Content
1. Dorothy Kowalski's funeral 0:00–3.44	Int. Catholic Church Walt is introduced as an embittered old man with outdated attitudes. It is obvious that the relationship with his two sons is rather cold and distant. Walt's granddaughter Ashley is inappropriately dressed. Father Janovich, a very young and inexperienced priest, delivers an impersonal eulogy.
2. After church 3:44–8:23	Int. Walt's House (same day) After the funeral service, the house is crowded with people. Walt does not know what to do with himself. Int. Cellar/Upstairs (same time) While Walt's grandsons intrude into his privacy by skimming through boxes in which they find photos and a medal from the Korean War, his granddaughter Ashley is obviously bored. Ext. Walt's House (evening) Walt leaves the funeral feast together with Daisy, stands outside and watches a whole crowd of Hmong people going into his next-door neighbors' house. His rude remark about the great number of people clearly shows him as a racist. Int. Garage (same time) Walt finds Ashley secretly smoking a cigarette. She wants to know what's going to happen to Walt's beloved car, a 1972 Ford Gran Torino, when he dies. At Walt's Door (later) Thao, a sixteen-year-old Hmong boy, asks for jumper cables but the old man slams the door in Thao's face. Father Janovich drops by and tries to persuade Walt to come for confession, but Walt tells him that he would not go to confession to a "boy that's just out of the seminary."

Plot

Scene	Content
3. Family conflicts (8:23–12:40)	Ext. Walt's House (later) / Int. Toyota Land Cruiser (same time) While Walt is helping two old ladies from the funeral with jumper cables to start their car, Mitch and his family leave. Although they know that Walt has worked at the local Ford factory for his entire life, they are annoyed about his reaction to their Japanese car. Int. Hmong House Next Door (same time) Phong, an old widow, complains about the fact that in contrast to their traditional values there is no man heading their household. Thao does not count in this respect as he does women's work and obeys to his sister. Ext. Walt's/Thao's House Walt looks with disdain at the house next door which – in contrast to his own – is in a poor state of repair. He comments on the fact that the neighborhood used to be Polish but has changed into a Hmong community. Parallel to Walt's complaints, Phong talks disparagingly about Walt, the only white man left in the neighborhood. Both Phong and Walt spit out simultaneously. Int. Walt's House (day) Father Janovich pays a visit to Walt, who does not conceal his dislike for the priest. In his opinion Janovich is only good at promising eternity to superstitious old ladies.
4. The Hmong gang (12:40–17:23)	Ext. Street (day) Thao is mocked at by Latino gang members to be an Asian woman. When a gang of Hmong youngsters appear, both gangs pull out their shotguns, but the Latinos give in and drive away. Spider, one of the leaders of the Hmong gang-bangers, is Thao's cousin and wants him to join their gang. Ext. Thao's House (day) Sue, Thao's sister, shows no fear in standing up to Spider and Smokie. But Thao is easily pressurized into becoming a gang member. As an initiation ritual, Thao has to steal Walt's Gran Torino.

Scene	Content
5. Life and death (17:23–20:04)	At the Bar (evening) Walt drinks together with his war buddies. Father Janovich enters the bar and tries to persuade Walt again to go to confession. In their talk about life and death it becomes obvious that Walt still suffers from the "horrible things" he did in the Korean War fifty years ago.
6. The initiation ritual fails (20:04–23:20)	Int. Walt's Bedroom / Garage (same night) Seeing a flashlight in his garage, Walt gets his military rifle. He does not recognize Thao. When Walt trips and falls to the ground, he accidentally fires a shot, but Thao escapes into the night. Int. Garage (afternoon) Mitch phones his father, hoping Walt might get him Lions season tickets by calling a friend of his. Walt does not tell him about the night's incident. Ext. Walt's Driveway (afternoon) Walt polishes the Gran Torino which is parked in the driveway. It is a provocative action, because he is daring the thief to come back.
7. Hero to the neighborhood (23:20–27:37)	Ext. Walt's Street (later that night) Smokie, Spider and their gang pull up at Thao's house. When they force Thao into their car, Sue and other family members try to fight them off. As the fighting spills into Walt's yard, he deters the Hmong gangbangers with his military rifle. As a consequence, they hastily drive away. Ext. Walt's Front Porch (next morning) Walt is considered to be the savior of the neighborhood. His porch is covered with presents from the Hmong community. Disrespecting the Hmong's gratefulness, Walt dumps the gifts in the trash. Ext. Walt's House (day) Following his mother's wish, Thao admits that he tried to steal the Gran Torino, for which he apologizes to Walt.

Plot

Scene	Content
8. Walt's bad conscience (27:37–30:23)	Int. Walt's Entryway (later that day) Father Janovich is standing on Walt's front step inviting him again to confess his sins. Walt tells him that "the thing that haunts a man the most is what he isn't ordered to do." Int. Old School Barbershop The ironic, but rude and offensive language between the Italian barber and Walt establishes the fact that they are old friends.
9. Walt saves Sue (30:23–34:48)	Ext. Sidewalk (same time) Sue and her white boyfriend Trey face serious trouble as they obviously infringed on African-American territory. Walt passes by in his pickup truck and saves Sue from harassment by a group of African-American gangbangers.
10. Foreshadowing forthcoming events (34:48–38:34)	Int. Walt's Pickup Truck (driving) Sue explains to Walt about Hmong culture, e.g. the different perspectives of Hmong men and women: "The girls go to college, the boys go to jail." Ext. Walt's Front Porch (early morning) It's Walt's birthday. His horoscope foreshadows the forthcoming events as it talks about making a choice between two life paths, second chances and an anticlimax.
11. Walt's birthday (38:48–41:57)	Int. Walt's Living Room (day) Ignoring Walt's physically and mentally sound condition, Mitch and Karen give him presents for people with restricted mobility "to make things a lot easier" and advise him to move to a nursing home. They are unceremoniously kicked out of Walt's house. Ext. Walt's Porch (evening) Walt celebrates his birthday on his own by having lots of Pabst beer cans, when Sue invites him over to their barbecue next door.

Scene Index

Scene	Content
12. Self-recognition (41:57–46:43)	Int. Thao's House (same time) Phong's angry outburst at Walt's presence makes Sue and others embarrassed. Sue teaches Walt about Hmong traditions. Int. Living Room (same time) The family's shaman reads Walt's mind. He is stunned at the shaman's knowledge about him as the wise man gives a true portrayal of Walt's failed life. Int. Bathroom (same time) Walt takes a long look at himself in the mirror. The shaman's words have led to an act of self-recognition, visualized by the reflection of Walt's face in the mirror.
13. Mingling with the Hmong (46:43–51:42)	Int. Kitchen (later) Walt enjoys tasting different Hmong dishes. Int. Basement (same time) The young Hmong have gathered in the basement. Sue takes Walt down there, and he seems to feel somewhat out of place. As he leans against the dryer, he realizes that the machine wobbles. So he looks under it to balance it out. Then he observes Youa fancying Thao, who sits passively in a corner. Walt begins to teach him how to act like a man, e.g. how to address women.
14. Thao's compensation (51:42–54:43)	Ext. Walt's Yard (day) Hmong women bring food and flower baskets. Walt is reluctant to accept the gifts but is more friendly than before. He starts to enjoy the Asian food. Ext. Walt's House (evening) Sue and her mother beg Walt to allow Thao to work off his debt in order to undo his dishonoring the family. It's obvious that it is not Thao's decision. Ext. Walt's Porch (next morning) Walt does not know what kind of jobs he should give Thao. The first tasks are absolutely senseless.

Plot

Scene	Content
15. Shaping up the neighborhood (54:43–58:35)	Ext. Walt's House / Neighborhood (next few days) Seeing a very dilapidated house across the street, Walt makes Thao shaping up the neighborhood. Despite the hard work and miserable conditions, he finally rises up to the tasks presented to him and renovates various houses under Walt's close scrutiny. Int. Walt's Bathroom/Entryway (morning) Walt spits blood into the sink. When Thao is ringing the doorbell, he gives him a day off.
16. Walt's fatal disease (58:35–1:01:44)	Int. Doctor's Office (day) Walt wonders about the absence of his regular doctor who has obviously retired years ago. He feels uncomfortable with the new Asian female doctor. Int. Mitch's Living Room (later) Walt calls his son who is busy with bills. Although Walt is seriously ill, he does not tell his son. Ext. Thao's Front Yard (day) When Spider and his gang pass the house, Walt points his hand like an imaginary gun at them.
17. Helping each other (1:01:43–1:07:48)	Int. Thao's Kitchen (morning) Thao asks Walt for help with the faucets in his house. Everything seems to be run-down and in need of repair. Int. Walt's Garage (a little later) Thao is impressed by all the tools. Their relation gets closer when he sees Walt coughing up blood again. Walt understands the circumstances of the initiation ritual. Int. Walt's Basement / Ext. Walt's Backyard (day) Walt can't get the freezer upstairs and asks Thao for help. Thao takes the lead. Walt then sells the freezer to him. Ext. Walt's Porch (day) Sue thanks Walt for being a role model for Thao.

Scene Index

Scene	Content
18. Manning up Thao (1:07:48–1:13:19)	Ext. Walt's Backyard (day) Thao is busy dong yard work. Talking about Thao's future, Walt sees a necessity in manning him up. He suggests a job as a construction worker. Int. Old School Barbershop (day) Walt and his friend Martin try and teach Thao to talk like a man.
19. Getting a job (1:13:19–1:16:47)	Ext. Construction Site / Int. Job Trailer (day) Walt and Thao walk up to the Office Trailer on the construction site to see the super. With Walt's help, Thao gets a job. The teenager is good at applying his recently acquired male language and behavior. Int. Walt's Truck / Hardware Store (later) Walt equips Thao with a tool belt for which the Hmong boy shall pay him back after getting his first paycheck.
20. Thao's punishment (1:16:47–1:19:30)	Ext. Bus Stop (afternoon) Smokie presses a lit cigarette into Thao's cheek as a punishment for his disobedience. Ext. Walt's Alley (morning) Walt gets aware of Thao's burn. Although Thao does not want him to do anything, Walt's reaction shows that he is about to do something in retaliation for the gang's violent act.
21. Retaliation and joy (1:19:30–1:24:42)	Ext. The Hmong Gangbangers' House (day) Walt kicks and beats Smokie hard, warning him to stay away from Thao. Ext. Walt's Backyard (day) Walt is enjoying himself with the Hmong neighbors; Thao has asked Youa out. Walt lets them take his Gran Torino for their date.

Plot

Scene	Content
22. Escalating violence (1:24:42–1:25:34)	Int. Walt's Living Room (evening) Walt is watching baseball when he witnesses gunfire in the direction of Thao's house coming from a van in the street. Ext. Thao's House (same time) Thao suffers from a cut at his neck, but the Hmong gangbangers deliberately aimed high with their guns so that nobody else is hurt; however, Sue is missing. When she returns home, she is heavily bleeding. Obviously, she has been brutally beaten and raped.
23. Walt's despair (1:25:34–1:29:39)	Int. Walt's House (later) In an act of auto-aggression Walt hurts himself smashing several pieces of furniture. His knuckles are bleeding, and he is sitting in a chair alone in the dark. When Father Janovich drops by to talk to him, Walt expresses his view that there will be no peace for Thao and Sue until the gang has gone away forever.
24. Preparations for his own death (1:29:39–1:32:33)	Int. Walt's Kitchen (morning) Thao cannot wait to kill Spider and his gangbangers, but Walt calms him down and tells him to come back at 4 o'clock. Int. Walt's Bathroom Walt enjoys having a bath. He smokes a cigarette for the first time in the house. Int. Barbershop Walt gets his hair cut. To the surprise of the barber he also wants to have a straight shave for the first time ever. Int. Men's Clothing Store Walt has a new suit tailored.

Scene	Content
25. An alarming confession (1:32:33–1:34:38)	Int. Catholic Church / Confessional Booth To Father Janovich's surprise, Walt wants to make a confession. However, he does not confess any severe sins, so the priest is alarmed about what he might do to the Hmong gang. Walt is finally at peace with himself.
26. Locking up Thao (1:34:38–1:39:29)	Int. Walt's Kitchen/Basement (3:51 p.m.) Walt tricks Thao into the basement and locks him up. He does not want the Hmong teenager to have blood on his hands. He confesses that he killed at least 13 Koreans, among them an innocent teenager of about Thao's age. Walt announces that he will "finish things" alone. Ext. Walt's House / Porch to Thao's House (same time) Despite animosities between Walt and Phong, the old man brings his dog Daisy to his neighbors' porch to make them look after her. Int. Bar (afternoon) Walt phones Sue, telling her to free her brother. Ext. The Gangbangers' House (afternoon) Father Janovich has called the police in order to prevent bloodshed. However, the police do not want to wait any longer as there is no evidence of any serious confrontation.
27. Walt's death (1:39:29–1:41:47)	Ext. The Gangbangers' House (evening) Walt provokes the Hmong gangbangers. When he tries to get out his lighter, he is shot by the nervous gang. While the Hmong gangbangers are arrested by the police, Thao and Sue arrive on the scene and are informed by an officer that Walt didn't even have a gun on him.

Plot

Scene	Content
28. Walt's funeral and his last will (1:41:47–1:46:30)	Int. Catholic Church (day) Walt's funeral takes place. Walt is dressed in his new suit. Sue and Thao are there in their traditional clothes as well as Walt's own family. Father Janovich admits that he had not known anything about life and death before he met Walt. Int. Law Office (day) According to Walt's last will, the Gran Torino goes to Thao on the condition that he doesn't modify it.
29. A new beginning (1:46:30–1:51:42)	On the Road (day) Thao is driving along Jefferson Avenue / Lake Shore Drive in Walt's Gran Torino together with Daisy on the front-passenger seat.

Exposition

> **INFO AT A GLANCE**
>
> **Introducing Walt Kowalski, his family, Father Janovich and the Hmong neighbors**
> - The plot starts on the day of Dorothy Kowalski's funeral which sets the tone and atmosphere of the beginning.
> - Walt Kowalski is introduced as a growling old man, unable to understand the changes around him and embittered by his loneliness.
> - The relation to his two sons Mitch and Steve is rather distanced.
> - Walt's grandchildren are presented as disrespectful teenagers with regard to their clothing and behavior.
> - Father Janovich, an inexperienced, young Catholic priest, delivers an impersonal eulogy. However, he is quite eager to fulfill his promise to Dorothy Kowalski to bring her husband to confession.
> - The neighboring Hmong family is introduced in a scene juxtaposed to Walt's funeral feast. In contrast to mourning the deceased, the Hmong celebrate the beginning of life of a new-born baby.
> - The 16-year-old Thao is portrayed as a shy young man who cannot live up to the role expectations of the future man in the house as he is ordered around by his sister, mother and grandmother.
> - Parallel to Walt's deeply rooted racial prejudices towards his neighbors, Phong, a widowed first-generation immigrant, cannot understand that Walt does not leave like all the other white Americans in the neighborhood.

The movie starts off with an unusual black-and-white version of the Warner Bros. icon, which sets the audience back in time to prepare the viewer for Walt Kowalski's anachronistic worldview. He still seems to live in the 1950s. The melancholy title song accompanying the black-and-white introductory pictures sets the tone for the opening scene. An establishing shot shows a Catholic church in an urban setting. Though impossible to recognize at this early stage, the whole story is set in Highland Park, a former middle-class neighborhood in Detroit, Michigan. With the dominant sound of an organ, the scene switches inside the church. A high-angle establishing shot shows a rather small congregation for Dorothy Kowalski's funeral, somehow lost in the quite enormous room. As the camera moves closer to the front of the church, passing the photo of the deceased, the audience gets a first glimpse of Walt. Quite symbolically, he is standing apart from the other visitors of the church service and is the only one next to Dorothy's coffin.

Black-and-white Warner Bros. icon

Sad music sets the tone for the opening scene

Walt's isolation

Plot

Disgust at Ashley's pierced belly button

His sullen facial expressions reveal not only the emotional burden of having lost his wife but also his general bitterness. When his grandchildren arrive, the viewer sees the sequence of events from Walt's point of view. Nothing escapes his hawk-like eyes which finally narrow on his granddaughter Ashley's bare and pierced belly button, triggering a snarling sound of disgust in him. In order to show his reaction, the director Clint Eastwood uses a medium close-up shot on his face.

Disrespectful grandchildren

To make things worse, Walt's oldest grandson Josh kneels down and mocks at the Catholic ritual of crossing oneself by saying: "Spectacles, testicles, wallet and watch." It is a quote from a popular joke.

> A woman was standing on a busy corner waiting for the crosswalk signal when an oncoming vehicle hit a car making a left turn.
> An elderly man stepped out of one car and immediately crossed himself (making the sign of the cross). The woman rushed over to help. When she reached the man, she asked if he was hurt. "No", came the reply.
> "Well, I think that it is wonderful that you gave thanks to God that you were unhurt."
> "What are you talking about?"
> "You made the sign of the cross when you got out of the car."
> "What sign of the cross?!" The man asked, and repeated the gesture, this time saying, "Spectacles, testicles, wallet and watch!"
> (www.beyondthescreen.com/sites/files/study_guide/Study_Guide_Gran_Torino_pdf)

Generation gap

While the other children (Ashley and Steve's two sons Daniel and David) laugh at this disrespectfulness, it remains unclear whether Walt has overheard the words as his face shows no direct reaction. However, this small scene introduces the generation gap within Walt's family.

Walt is "still living in the '50s"

With a panning shot, the scene switches to a conversation between Walt's two sons. Obviously, Ashley's father Mitch has witnessed Walt's reaction to his daughter's clothing, but – surprisingly – does not find his daughter's naked belly inappropriate. He is rather annoyed by the old man's conservative attitude. For his brother it is clear that Walt is "still living in the '50s", hopelessly backward and unable to accept any change. For this reason, there have been continuous, inevitable conflicts with their father. As a consequence, they have kept a distance, e.g. stopped celebrating Thanksgiving together. Neither of them wants Walt to live at their home. When the camera turns to the old man again, the audience sees him coughing, which introduces the topic of Walt's serious, maybe even fatal disease (lung cancer).

Walt's inner distance to his sons Mitch and Steve

In the following eulogy, Father Janovich talks about life and death, offering different interpretations of death as an end or a new beginning. Despite Walt's close relationship with Dorothy, Father Janovich delivers a rather impersonal speech. As a very young priest, he has presumably no idea about the pains caused by death and by losing a beloved partner. His apparent inexperience in giving consolation to people of Walt's generation is additionally strengthened by his visible detachment from the congregation. The eulogy is disturbed by a beeping on Ashley's cell phone. She seems to be a selfish person without any regard for the feelings of others.

Father Janovich's impersonal speech

When the scenery changes to Walt's house for the funeral feast, everybody seems to be busy. There is no shared mourning, no sense of community. The low-key lighting of the whole scene fits to the rather tense atmosphere. The widower himself does not know what to do with himself so he is quite happy to find himself the task of getting some extra chairs from the basement.

No sense of community at the funeral feast

Meanwhile his grandsons Josh, Daniel and David intrude on his privacy when they open a box with private photos and other pieces of memory. Eastwood allows the audience only a quick glance at a black-and-white picture from the Korean War (1950–1953) with young Walt, behind him several bodies sprawled dead on the ground. The photo, however, and the Silver Star medal are necessary to establish Walt's essential experience. As Walt appears, the grandsons feel found out and try to look innocent. It is significant that not a single word is exchanged between them. Ashley is obviously bored and loudly expresses her worries about being disconnected from the Internet. Her embarrassed parents have to tell

Walt's Korean War experience

No communication

her that she should help her grandfather with the chairs. However, Walt is unable to accept any help, the least from his granddaughter to whom he seems to have no relation at all.

Walt's racism

Another side of Walt Kowalski is shown when he flees from the feast and goes into the yard with his Labrador Daisy. Standing outside his house, he can see flocks of Asian people pouring into his next-door neighbor's home. On account of his rhetoric question "How many swamp rats can you get in one room?" one has to conclude that he is a racist. To undermine his words, he spits out.

Sometime later Walt detects Ashley secretly smoking a cigarette in his garage. Corresponding to the tension between the two characters, Eastwood uses a very low-key lighting. The teenager has spotted her grandfather's Gran Torino, which is a "cool old car" for her. For him, it is his "baby" since it rolled off the assembly line in 1972. With shocking explicitness she asks Walt what will happen to it when he dies. In the same context she wonders whether she might get the "super cool retro couch" as part of her furniture for her room when going to college. For good reason, Walt is appalled by her behavior, as a consequence of which he walks out of the garage without any comment. However, his spitting out symbolically shows his contempt for her.

The "cool old car"

Ashley's demands and expectations

In this emotionally difficult state of mind, Walt is confronted with two unexpected visitors. Thao, the 16-year-old Hmong neighbor, asks for jumper cables. While Walt is standing in the dark light of the house's interior, expressing his dark mood, Thao is seen in full daylight. The widower does not conceal his racist attitude and calls him a "zipperhead" before he slams the door in Thao's face.

Dark lighting expresses Walt's mood

Turning around, Walt faces Father Janovich who tries hard to befriend him. However, his strategy of calling him "Walt" fails, as the old man insists on being called "Mr. Kowalski". As promised to Dorothy, Father Janovich wants Walt to come for confession. With overt aggression conveyed by close-up shots of Walt's face, he confesses that he never cared for church and only went there because of his wife. Apart from that, he shows his contempt for the young priest by saying that he would not "confess to a boy that's just out of the seminary."

The introduction of the Hmong neighbors is deliberately set in two parallel scenes of a family party. However, in contrast to Walt's funeral feast, the Hmong celebrate the beginning of a new life. The juxtaposition of the two scenes is made obvious by the simultaneousness of Walt's guests leaving and the Hmong visitors arriving.

Parallel party scenes

In contrast to Walt's rejection of Thao's request for jumper cables, Walt himself has to help two old white ladies with their dead battery. In this moment his son Mitch and his family pull up in their white Toyota Land Cruiser. As a poor excuse for their early leaving Mitch tells his father that the children are "getting restless." The truth behind that is that they have nothing in common anymore and leave before new inevitable conflicts arise. An old one is Mitch's choice of a Japanese car which does not correspond to Walt's worldview ("Kill you to buy American"). Walt has worked at the local Ford factory for his entire life, so it is bitter for him to see his son buying a Toyota – particularly on the background of the severe financial crisis in 2008 which nearly led to a breakdown of the U.S. automobile industry.

Mitch's Toyota Land Cruiser

Walt's Ford career

Switching back to the Hmong neighbors, the party over there starts off in a brighter atmosphere in the backyard. The lighting is different, as the sun is shining now and the guests seem to enjoy themselves. Some are watching the ritual beheading of a chicken by the shaman, which only confirms Walt's racial prejudice that they are all "barbarians".

Lighter atmosphere in the sun

Despite the relaxed atmosphere outside, there are problems discussed inside. Phong, a widowed first-generation immigrant, wants her daughter to get married again. In her traditional view there has to be a man heading the house. The teenager Thao cannot match up with these role expectations. He lacks self-confidence and – according to Phong – is ordered around by the women in

Thao's difficulty in matching up with male role expectations

Hmong traditions strengthen community

the house, in particular his sister Sue. To underline her words, the audience witnesses Thao washing the dishes which is considered to be women's work in Hmong tradition. He is contrasted by another man just leaving his plate next to the sink. In remarkable contrast to the funeral feast next door, the Hmong experience a sense of community. The local shaman has assembled all guests for a blessing ceremony for the recently born baby. The old traditions are obviously kept alive.

Walt's well-kept property in a run-down neighborhood

A high-angle establishing shot indicates a new scene. Walt is cleaning his driveway with a broom. In contrast to the home next door, Walt's whole property, including the front lawn, is accurately kept. When he looks with disdain at the peeling paint and the neglected lawn, he is reminded of the times in which Highland Park used to be a nice white neighborhood. Like Walt Kowalski, a lot of the inhabitants were from Poland, including Polarski, the previous owner of the neighboring house.

Mutual hatred and racial prejudices

Parallel to Walt's xenophobic comment – his terms for the Asian immigrants are "chinks" and "slopes" – Phong calls him a "dumb rooster" in her own language which Walt does not understand. Walt seems to be the last white man in an all-Asian neighborhood. Both Phong and Walt hate each other. When she sees him spit out as a gesture of contempt, she spits out a mouthful of betel nut juice.

Walt keeps Father Janovich at a distance

In the final scene of the exposition, Father Janovich again tries to fulfill his promise to look after Walt. It is a conversation on the doorstep, the Korean veteran stands inside the dark hallway while the priest remains outside. This position is quite symbolic, as Walt keeps the clergyman at a distance. He does not want to let him in, disturbing his privacy. The old man is definitely not at peace with himself which is indicated by the low-key lighting inside. Father Janovich, on the other hand, seems to offer some light at the end of the tunnel. However, the Catholic priest fails again. Walt briskly tells him to go, calling him an "over-educated, 27-year-old virgin who likes to hold hands of old ladies who are superstitious and promises them eternity."

Gang Pressure on Thao

INFO AT A GLANCE

Temptation and resistance
- Thao is molested by a Latino gang when his cousin Spider and the Hmong gang appear. Both gangs provoke each other, until the Latinos give in, when Smokie shows his machine gun.
- Spider and Smokie want Thao to join their gang. While Sue stands up to the gangbangers, Thao is easily pressurized into becoming a member.
- As an initiation ritual Thao should steal the Gran Torino but when Walt wakes up, gets his rifle to confront the thief in the garage, Thao runs away.
- In a conversation with Father Janovich at the Veteran's bar, Walt reveals that he is still haunted by the "horrible things" he did in the Korean War.
- In a final attempt, the Hmong gangbangers try to take Thao by force. In an act of self-defense Walt takes his military rifle from Korea and makes them flee.

A long shot through a wire fence establishes a new scene in which Thao strolls along a deserted street reading a book. In his sandals and socks he definitely does not look very masculine. Spanish rap announces a gang of Latinos in their blue Chevrolet. Obviously they consider reading a female activity, because they slow down and mock at Thao, asking him whether he is a boy or a girl. The Hmong teenager listens to the Latinos, he even laughs about them, but is smart enough not to answer any of the ongoing racist provocations.

Provocations of the Latino gang

When Spider, Thao's cousin, detects his younger relative, he and his fellow Hmong gangbangers want to protect him. As they approach in their white souped-up Honda both gangs start yelling at each other. Interestingly enough, Spider asks the Latinos why they do not go back to their own country. At first Eastwood uses a tracking shot to have both cars in the picture. Their colors form a stark contrast. As the tension heats up, he switches to close shots showing either the Latinos or the Hmong. A Latino in the background is the first to produce a shotgun, indicating that the situation might get out of control. However, as Smokie pulls a machine gun, the Latinos give in and drive away. It is obvious that Thao has abandoned his humorous reaction to the Latinos, when Spider tells him to get into the car. He knows that

Hmong gang with Thao's cousin Spider

Dangerous confrontation

this might be more serious than before. But he resists the temptation and continues his own way.

Playing with gender concepts

As promised, the Hmong gangbangers turn up at Thao's house the next day. Eastwood juxtaposes different gender concepts in this scene. Thao, sitting on the ground in front of the house, is busy gardening. That's the reason for Spider's question why he is doing women's work. In contrast to him, Sue has obviously time for leisurely pastimes, and is reading a journal on the stairs. The 17-year-old Sue seems to be a tough, self-confident woman, as she laughs about her cousin's newly adopted name Spider (his original name is Fong). Additionally, she is not afraid to stand up to Smokie. The Hmong gangbanger asks her for her age, wondering whether she might be able to fulfill his sexual desires, which foreshadows her rape later in the movie. Sue tells him that she is mentally "way too old" for him. However, obviously she feels uneasy about the situation because she immediately goes inside.

Sue stands up to the gangbangers

Low-angle camera makes the gang seem more threatening

Now Thao is easily pressurized by the Hmong gangbangers. It is noteworthy that most of the scene is filmed from a very low angle, probably just off the ground. With Thao sitting on the grass, the other young men seem to be more threatening, as they tower over him. When Thao finally rises, he has achieved an equal rank and, symbolically, has become a member of the gang. Thao knows that he has to do something as an initiation ritual. Although he knows that this is not the right thing – what one can deduct from his facial expression when all of them stand in the driveway – he accepts the challenge.

Racial jokes at the Veteran's bar

Meanwhile Walt enjoys the evening with his buddies in the Veteran's bar. He is telling a racist joke when Father Janovich appears for another attempt to bring him to confession. Walt is impressed by his persistence, so he offers him some private talk. The priest is literally forced into having an alcoholic drink, a fact which is of interest later in the movie. Talking about life and death, the topic of Janovich's eulogy, Walt criticizes Father Janovich for having no idea of the things he is talking about. He is convinced that he knows a lot more about death, as he

Life and death

fought in the Korean War for three years. There he and others had

> "shot men, stabbed them with bayonets, hacked seventeen-year-olds to death with shovels. Stuff I'll remember till the day I die. Horrible things, but things I live with." (19:17)

Walt is haunted by what he did in the Korean War

Obviously he is still haunted by what he did 50 years ago. Being asked what he knows about life, Walt has no convincing answer. He vaguely admits that he is not good at leading a fulfilled life. Against his will, he has begun to let his mask fall a bit. The camera supports this turning-point by showing the faces of Walt and Father Janovich in detail. While most of the scene is filmed in over-the-shoulder and reverse shots, in the end the intimacy of the situation is covered by zooming-in close-ups.

Turning-point in the relation between Walt and Father Janovich

Later that same night Walt wakes up from some noise in his garage. A flashlight from within makes him get his 30-06 M1 Garand Rifle he took home from Korea. For him it is a war-like situation at home which is supported by the low drum sounds in the background. As he enters the garage, it is quite dark. This is a very realistic setting which creates suspense, because the viewer does not know what will happen next. Walt hits a small lamp which consequently swings around, causing additional confusion. However, he seems to have focused on his target. It is Thao, but Walt does not recognize him.

Confusing light and music create suspense

When Walt comes nearer, Thao backs away, his eyes wide with terror. Barely visible, the young man trips over some tool box which causes a chain reaction as a result of which Walt falls to the ground as well. Fast cuts and an unsteady hand-held camera fit in perfectly with the unclear situation. In falling, Walt accidentally fires a shot but hits a metal beer sign on the wall only. Thao gets up first and flees, past the Korean War veteran and the Hmong gangbangers who have waited outside in their car. Walt is not hurt either, but remains lying on the ground, shocked and exhausted. He finally coughs up some blood, a sign of the seriousness of his physical condition.

Fast cuts with a hand-held camera

Coughing up blood

Plot

Failed communi-
cation between
Walt and Mitch

Obviously the following afternoon (Walt fixes some screen mesh on the interior of the garage's windows) his son Mitch calls. The camera intercuts between Walt's garage and Mitch's huge, modern suburban house. Usually Mitch only calls when he wants something from his father, so Walt suspiciously asks him about his request. In a sarcastic side-remark he additionally explains that there is no more to get from him after Mitch's wife has gone through all of Dorothy's jewelry. Mitch, however, pretends that he is just interested whether his father is fine. This would have been the perfect time for Walt to inform his son about last night's failed burglary, but he seems unwilling to bother him. At last, Mitch comes to the real reason for his call, namely his wish to get tickets for the Detroit Lions, the local football team. Obviously Walt used to know someone who has seasonal tickets for him. But he just hangs up without replying anything.

Challenging the
thief

Later that day one can see Walt rubbing Turtle Wax on the Gran Torino. It is not just polishing a car, it is an activity full of emotional pride which is underlined by the title music. He has parked the car in the front area of his driveway, daring the thief to come back. Sparklingly as it shines, it is a temptation, a challenge.

The 1972 Ford Gran Torino

However, the Hmong do not come back that night to steal the Gran Torino, but to grab Thao. Sue, her mother and her grandmother do their best to protect him. Even a male neighbor comes to fight the gangbangers off. The following turmoil is filmed with a hand-held camera again, which reveals only details of the ongoing fighting. Sometimes the camera is positioned just above the ground, so that only legs of the actors can be seen. These effects are deliberately chosen to create suspense.

As the fighting spills into Walt's yard, having already destroyed one of his garden goblins, the old man acts out of self-defense. The camera moves upwards, on the one hand emphasizing Walt's height – he is in fact taller than the Hmong gangbangers. On the other hand, the camera follows the perspective of the fighters who seem to lie more or less on the ground when Walt appears with his rifle. The camera stays in a low-angle point of view, thus making him seem more powerful.

<small>Low-angle camera stresses Walt's power</small>

Smokie warns Walt not to "fuck" with him, but the Korean War ex-soldier calmly orders him: "Get off my lawn!" In order to strengthen his authority, he boasts with his war-time experience by saying: "We used to stack fucks like you five feet high in Korea and used you for sandbags." Low drum sounds combined with some dramatic music underline the dead-seriousness of the situation. Finally the Hmong gangbangers accept their inferiority in that moment and leave angrily.

<small>"Get off my lawn!"</small>

<small>Drum sounds</small>

Hero to the Neighborhood

INFO AT A GLANCE

Savior against his will
- Walt's porch is covered with presents from the Hmong community. Disrespecting the Hmong's gratefulness, he dumps the gifts in the trash.
- Thao admits having tried to steal the Gran Torino.
- Walt suffers most from the deeds he was not ordered to do in Korea.
- He saves Sue from harassment by a group of African Americans.
- Sue teaches Walt about Hmong history and culture. In her view Hmong "girls go to college and the boys go to jail."

Plot

Prepared for acts of retaliation

Walt seems to expect some acts of retaliation for what happened so he did not lock up his rifle again. The scene starts with him having the rifle prepared in his kitchen. To his utmost surprise, there are no gangbangers coming up his porch, but other Hmong people thanking him for saving Thao. His porch is covered with fruit baskets, flowers and other presents. Sue and her family offer him perennials, i.e. plants that "come back every year." Symbolically, they want to express some ever-lasting thanks to him. For them Walt is the "hero to the neighborhood", as Sue explains to him, for he is the first who has done something against the gangbangers pestering the Hmong community.

Reasons for the Hmong's gratefulness

Walt does not understand the situation and just wants to be left alone

A close-up of Walt's face shows that he is disgusted at the Hmong's gratefulness and dumps all gifts in the trash. Self-centered as he is, he does not understand the inappropriateness of his actions and just wants to be left alone. Thao looks down on the ground when he is confronted with Walt. Obviously, he finds it difficult to admit that he tried to steal the Gran Torino. When he finally apologizes, Walt does not accept that but warns him with outspoken aggression: "Let me tell you something, boy, you step on this property again, you're done."

Father Janovich does not accept Walt's explanations

Father Janovich heard about the troubles of the previous night. When he criticizes Walt for not calling the police, the veteran falls back into his old pattern. Making fun of the padre, he pretends to have prayed that they might show up. Earnestly he argues that it was a situation comparable to his war experience in Korea where he had to act all by himself. However, this time the priest does not want to let him off with his usual explanation of life based on the 1950s. Being confronted with the fact that they are not in Korea now, Walt does not know what to say. An awkward pause arises. Father Janovich offers him forgiveness for the things he was ordered to do, so he might be at peace with himself in the end. Walt, however, reveals that "the thing that haunts a man the most is what he isn't ordered to do."

Walt's guilt

The following short scene introduces Walt's barber Martin, a second-generation Italian immigrant. Walt is having his regular haircut in the old-fashioned barbershop once in three weeks. He and Martin seem to be very familiar with each other, as they are using a lot of swearwords in their funny dialogue. Walt calls the Italian man a "Wop-Dago" and "dipshit", whereas the barber uses the address "Pollack son of bitch" and "prick". In another context an observer might think that they are very rude to each other, but for the two of them it is rather a ritualized game they play.

<small>Exchanging swearwords with the Italian barber Martin</small>

Walt's image as a hero to the neighborhood is underlined in the next scene in which he saves Sue from some African American men. The scene is set in a run-down neighborhood which the African Americans call their "territory". Sue and her date Trey, a white teenager with big baggy pants and a sports-cap turned backwards, have tried to use a shortcut for buying CDs when they bump into three black guys. Trey tries to play down the dangerous situation by making a joke and calling the African Americans "bro" – a stereotypical term used within the black community. However, the African Americans are only amused by his strategy, flip his cap onto the ground and begin pushing him around. Trey is too afraid to show any resistance.

<small>African-American "territory"</small>

<small>Trey's strategy of calling the African Americans "bro"</small>

Walt happens to pass by in his white pickup truck and watches the scene from a distance. He witnesses the African Americans encircling Sue and grabbing her by the arm. Their body language as well as their words indicate that they aim at sexually harassing her. The Hmong girl is extremely courageous. She tries to use her intellectual superiority and confronts the African Americans with their stereotypical behavior ("another asshole who has a fetish for Asian girls? God, it gets so old"; "Of course, right to the stereotype thesaurus: Call me a 'whore' and a 'bitch' in the same sentence").

<small>Walt witnesses the scene from his truck</small>

<small>Sue's intellectual superiority</small>

Most of the time, the scene is filmed from a low-angle point of view. This not only reflects Sue's perspective, as there is quite a difference in height between the Hmong teenager and the black men. More importantly, this cinematic device makes the African Americans more menacing (see e.g. picture on p. 28).

<small>Low-angle camera</small>

Plot

When they start pushing her around and the situation might get serious, Walt pulls up. To the surprise of the three men, he gets out of his truck. With his usual sign of contempt, he spits out. He pulls out an imaginary gun and shoots with his fingers at the African Americans. They are confused but do not allow Sue to get into Walt's truck. As his previous strategy has failed, Walt then produces a real gun to reinforce his demand. At the same time the drum sounds set in to underline the dramatic effect. This time, the African Americans comply with his request and let Sue go. On their way home Walt starts giving her a lecture, in which he strongly criticizes Sue for risking her life by taking that route. Furthermore, he recommends her to quit the relation with the useless Trey. In his opinion, she should mingle with her own kind.

Walt's lecture

That is the clue for Sue to inform him about Hmong history and culture. They are an ethnic group scattered over Laos, Thailand and China. In the Vietnam War, the Hmong allied with the Americans, as a consequence of which they had to leave their countries after the American defeat. Lutherans brought them to the Midwest.

Hmong history and culture

Being asked about her brother Thao, she tells Walt about the different perspectives of male and female Hmong:

Perspectives of Hmong girls and boys

> "It's really common. Hmong girls over here fit in better. The girls go to college and the boys go to jail." (36:39)

28

In her opinion, Thao is quite smart, but he has not got a role model and no instruction which way to go. At the end of the scene Walt's and Sue's equal level is also expressed by the camera which takes high and low angle positions during their ride to create the illusion that both actors are of similar size.

Painful Self-Recognition

> **INFO AT A GLANCE**
>
> **Walt's birthday**
> - Walt's horoscope foreshadows the forthcoming events.
> - Mitch and his wife Karen are ignorant of the inappropriateness of their birthday presents.
> - The Hmong shaman offers Walt some deep insight into himself. In an act of self-recognition, he realizes that he has got more in common with his Hmong neighbors than with his own family.
> - When he mingles with the young Hmong in the basement, he starts teaching Thao, e.g. how to address women.

Walt's reading the paper on his birthday informs the audience about the things to come. The horoscope especially attracts his attention which he reads aloud to himself:

> "Your birthday today. Daisy! This year, you have to make a choice between two life paths. Second chances come your way. Extraordinary events culminate in what might seem to be an anticlimax." (37:11)

Walt's horoscope

While most horoscopes are rather vague, this one seems to hit the bull's eye. By helping Thao and his family Walt indeed is offered a second chance to atone for his war crimes. Given the roles Clint Eastwood used to take in former films, Walt's death as some kind of martyr serves like an unexpected anticlimax in the end.

Shortly afterwards another small scene foreshadows the forthcoming events. Sitting on his porch, Walt watches an elderly white lady struggling to unload her groceries from her car. When her bag rips, three teenagers happen to walk past her and laugh at her spilled items instead of lending her a hand. Understandably, the old man asks himself: "What the hell is it with kids nowadays?"

Plot	
Thao helps a neighbor	However, to his surprise, Thao turns up and helps the old lady, which Walt really appreciates. For him it is a first sign that the young Hmong has a good heart.
Mitch's and Karen's misjudgment	About midday Mitch and Karen have come to visit Walt on his birthday. Obviously they think that he is unable to deal with his daily chores, so they bring presents "to make things a lot easier", e.g. a gopher (a tool for people who are unable to bend down and reach things) or a phone with really big numbers. To make things worse, they have brought along brochures about retirement homes. All this suggests that in their opinion Walt is restricted in his physical abilities and no longer able to live the life he used to live. None of that is true, of course. It is perfectly understandable that their embarrassing misjudgment leads to Walt kicking them out of the house.
Walt's birthday celebration	As a consequence, Walt celebrates his birthday on his own, sitting on the porch and drinking his favorite local beer (Pabst). In the evening Sue persuades him to come to their family barbecue. Because of his loneliness and the fact that there is no beer left, Walt comes to the conclusion that he "might as well drink with strangers than drink alone" and accompanies her. Sue obviously started to like him, which can also be observed from the nickname "Wally" she uses. Not surprisingly, Walt does not like that, because he does not want to get any closer. In his white conservative worldview he has got nothing in common with these Asian immigrants.
"Wally"	
Phong's disapproval of Walt's coming	For apparent reasons Walt immediately draws the other guests' attention to himself which makes him a little bit uneasy. To the embarrassment of the other visitors, Phong does not conceal her disapproval of Walt's coming. Although she speaks in Hmong, Walt understands that she hates him and does not like him being there. He tries to be as friendly as possible, but everything he does offends the Hmong. His strategy to look the others in the eyes, is considered rude in their culture. Like American parents do with their children, Walt pats a little girl on her head. All guests are shocked. Sue explains to him that in Hmong tradition one should never do that because people believe that the soul resides in the head.
Cultural traps	

The family's shaman Kor Khue offers Walt to "read" him. Astonishingly, he is able to give a precise analysis of the old man's psyche. Sue translates:

> "He says that people do not respect you. They don't even wanna look at you. […] He says the way you live, your food has no flavor. You're worried about your life. […] You made a mistake in your past life, like a mistake that you did you're not satisfied with. […] He says you have no happiness in your life. It's like you're not at peace." (44:42)

The shaman's precise analyis of Walt's psyche

Walt is stunned at the truth of the shaman's words. When he begins to realize their meaning, the camera slowly zooms into his face. The close-ups reveal that he is hit by an unexpected insight. He gets up and standing in the middle of the room, is quite pale and has to breathe hard. For some seconds he watches the old Hmong people being served tea by some of the younger ones. This is exactly what it should be like in Walt's opinion and what he misses in his own family. However, his coughing up blood, which can be seen from a close-up of his hand, brings him back to himself. He tries to hide the blood stains from Sue but she starts worrying about him and follows him to the bathroom upstairs.

Shocked by an unexpected insight

Respect for the old

Alone there Walt has to admit to himself:

> "God, I've got more in common with these gooks than I do my own spoilt rotten family. Jesus Christ. Happy birthday!" (46:15)

Common values with Hmong people

This shocking introspection is perfectly visualized by Walt's looking at himself in the mirror. It is a turning-point in his life. Metaphorically, the reference to his birthday might stand for a new beginning. Though still troubled by the "horrible things" in his past and his racial prejudices, he begins to regard the Hmong neighbors as friends, as people he is somehow connected to.

Visualized introspection as a turning-point

The consequences of this change can be seen immediately. Walt dives into the unknown culture to an extent hardly imaginable before. He really enjoys being fed by some old Hmong ladies in the kitchen. His good mood is more than obvious. Very unusual for him, he even makes jokes. Sue's idea of mingling, however, goes beyond

Joyful mingling with the Hmong

tasting Hmong hot dishes. She takes him down to the basement where the young Asians have gathered.

Difficult situation in the basement

For apparent reasons, this is not Walt's world. He could be their grandfather, so he stands apart not knowing what to do. The whole scene is filmed in a very low-key lighting, which can be interpreted as a sign of Walt's emotionally difficult situation down there. Leaning against the dryer, he realizes that the machine wobbles. Practical as he is, he gets down on his knees, looks under it and adjusts the short leg underneath to balance out the machine. All the Hmong youngsters watch Walt, obviously trying not to laugh.

Balancing out the dryer

Focus on Walt, Thao and Youa

Although there are quite a few people in the room, the camera focuses on Walt, Thao and a young woman called Youa. Thao sits alone, he is in a bad mood. The presence of his old neighbor does not make it any better. The Hmong girl is surrounded by group of young men in the center of the basement, but Walt observes that she looks at Thao over and over again with a charming smile. Thao has noticed her but shyly looks away. Obviously Youa is bored by the other teenagers, so she talks to Walt, before she finally leaves the room, followed by her admirers.

Youa's looks at Thao

"Toad" instead of Thao

This is the moment when Walt starts teaching Thao. He calls him "Toad" ('Kröte'), which indicates that the process of appreciating him as an individual human being has not yet even started. However, without any necessity he gives him some pieces of advice about how to deal with women. From his personal experience, Walt knows that a man has to "work at" getting a partner. In his typical grumpy way he scolds the teenager for his passiveness:

Criticizing Thao for his passiveness

> "I knew you were a dipshit the first time I ever saw you ... but I never thought you were worse with women than you are at stealing cars, Toad. […] You're blowing it with that girl who was there. Not that I give a shit about a toad like you. […] I may not be the most pleasant person to be around with but I got the best woman who was ever on that planet to marry me. I worked at it. […] But you, you know, you're letting Click Clack, Ding Dong and Charlie Chan just walk out with Miss

What's-her-Face. She likes you, you know? Though I don't know why. […] She's been looking at you all day, stupid." (50:20–51:13)

According to Walt, the reason for Thao's attitude is that he is a "big fat pussy", meaning that he does not act like a man. In his opinion, Thao's passiveness rather fits the role of a woman.

Thao does not act like a man

Teaching Thao (How) to Become a Man

> **INFO AT A GLANCE**
>
> **Walt and Thao are becoming friends**
> - Thao has to work off his guilt to undo his dishonoring of the family.
> - Walt makes him shape up the whole neighborhood. It is the first time that the young Hmong teenager is able to rise to tasks presented to him.
> - Despite the doctor's (presumably) fatal diagnosis of lung cancer, Walt does not tell his son Mitch about it.
> - When Spider and his gang pass Thao's house, Walt points his hand like an imaginary gun at them.
> - He and Thao help each other (faucets, freezer).
> - Sue thanks Walt that he has become a role model for her brother.
> - Walt und Martin try to teach Thao about how men talk to each other.
> - With the old man's help, Thao gets a job in construction.

A close-up of Walt mowing his lawn does not only indicate a new scene, but again shows the old white man's typical activity of maintaining his own property. Obviously some time has elapsed. Hmong women keep on bringing food and flowers to Walt's porch. He would definitely prefer that they stop to show their gratefulness but the smell of the hitherto unknown Asian food makes him weak. His question to one woman whether one of the dishes is "that chicken-dumpling thing" she brought "the other day" indicates his new ability to differentiate between the offered food. In a wider context this means that he has become more familiar with the Hmong culture, as a result of which he is now unable to decline their offerings.

Maintaining his own property

Growing familiarity with Hmong culture

Thao's mother wants her son to make amends for his attempt to steal the Gran Torino. Together with her children, she is waiting for Walt on the steps of his porch.

Making amends

Low-angle camera reveals the Hmong's contemporary dominance	Filmed from a low-angle point of view, they seem to be taller than the white man. Symbolically, this conveys the idea that they are more powerful in that moment than Walt, which is, in fact, true.
Family hierarchy	Against the veteran's will, they are successful in persuading him to accept their wishes. The teenager does not like the idea at all, but has to comply with his mother's and sister's order. The family's hierarchy is as well shown by the low-angle camera position in front of the porch. The camera takes up Thao's point of view when both women scold him in Hmong to shut up.
Thao's inferior position	The same camera perspective is used for the following day, when Thao starts his work. Walt towers above him on his porch, while Thao is shown standing small and powerless on his front step. Walt does not really know what to do with the 16-year-old boy, so he gives him the senseless task of counting the birds in a tree. However, when he sees a very dilapidated house just across the street, he has the idea of getting Thao to shape up the run-down neighborhood. This is primarily motivated by
Walt's motivation	the fact that he is fed up with having to look at the neglected houses for years.
Thao rises to the given challenges	Thao fixes a roof, scrapes the paint at his own house, reattaches house numbers, digs out a big tree stump and removes a wasp nest. It is hard work but satisfying which one can conclude from the fact that he is quite happy when he asks for more work on his last day. Obviously, it is the first time in his life that he has been given tasks challenging him as a man.
Dissolves instead of clear cuts	In the movie, the period of the week in which Thao works off his guilt lasts only a very short time. In contrast to the dominant clear cuts between the scenes throughout the movie, Eastwood here uses dissolves to indicate the lapse of time. The underlying sentimental music supports Thao's emotionally important development.
Walt realizes that he is seriously ill	With another attack of coughing up blood Walt has to face the fact that he is probably seriously ill. His worried look into the mirror indicates a second moment of self-

recognition. This leads to the bad mood he is in when he opens the door on Thao's final day. The Hmong teenager has done enough so Walt gives him a day off. Thao's face reveals that he is disappointed and does not understand Walt's reaction. As he is about to go, the old man presumably wants to thank him for his work or express his appreciation for Thao's achievement, but he is unable to. A close-up of Walt's face shows his emotional conflict, in which his old prejudiced self finally takes over.

Unable to express any thanks

An establishing shot of a waiting-room at the doctor's takes the viewer to the next scene. Walt is obviously confused by the multicultural mix of people around him. He is the only white person in the room. It gets even worse when a Muslim woman calls his name, but cannot pronounce it correctly. It turns out that his regular (white) doctor, Dr. Feldman, retired three years ago, and a female Asian, Dr. Chu, took over. The mentioned time-span reveals that Walt – typical of most men – has not seen his doctor for quite a long time.

Multicultural crowd at the doctor's

The results of the medical tests are not presented directly, but can be deducted from the next scene in which Walt phones his son Mitch. The low-key lighting reflects the veteran's inner despair. It is never mentioned in the movie what the doctor's diagnosis is. However, due to Walt's chain smoking and his coughing up blood one has to assume that he suffers from terminal lung cancer. The medical documents Walt keeps on looking at are barely visible to the audience. On closer inspection there is to be seen a "Hospital Admittance Form" which indicates that he is urgently recommended to go to hospital.

Unknown diagnosis

Hospital Admittance Form

Based on this context, it is natural to guess that Walt wants to tell his son about his problems. However, it is quite an effort for him, so he starts the conversation by asking over and over again whether everybody is fine. Alternatively, one might assume that he is not sure whether he should bother his son with his actual situation since he has never done so. It just might be a single helpless attempt to get into closer touch with him. Anyhow, the phone call takes a bad turn when

Mitch is busy with bills	Mitch tells him that he is busy with bills. For the emotionally distressed father (cf. the close-up of his facial expressions) it is the proof that there is no connection between him and his family, that they have no time for him and do not show any interest in him. The melancholy sound of the title song is added to the scene in order to make the audience share Walt's feelings.
"This kid doesn't have a chance"	The story then turns back to Thao's problems. On one of the following days the Hmong gang passes his house in their white Honda. Like in other scenes, loud rap music announces their arrival before the audience is provided with a shot of the car. Standing on his porch, Walt comments to himself that "this kid doesn't have a chance." As a warning, he holds out his right hand like a gun, pointing at the Hmong youngsters. As if firing, he moves his thumb several times. Smokie comments that with a rude gesture, warning him to mind his own business. Until now, they exchange threats only but it is made clear that the implicit violence will escalate one day.
Thao's house is falling apart	Another problem Thao faces is the state his family's home is in. On closer look, everything inside seems to fall apart. The young Hmong asks his old neighbor for help with a faucet. Eastwood uses a series of low-angle shots in this context. This nicely corresponds not only to Walt's perspective when he is lying on the kitchen floor, but also to the look at the ceiling with the wobbly fan. Both things are then fixed in Walt's garage. Thao is impressed by the old man's tools. This is the moment
Taking Thao under his wing	when Walt starts to take the teenager under his wing to "man him up". He supplies him with a starter set with which "any man who's worth his salt can do half the household chores."

Their new relation is also expressed by their mutual addressing of personal matters. When Thao witnesses Walt coughing up blood again, he strongly advises him to see a doctor. The Korean War veteran, on the other hand, for the first time asks Thao for information about the background of his problem with the Hmong gang.

He now seems to understand how Thao was talked into stealing the Gran Torino as an initiation. His sympathy for the teenager can also be seen from his rare smiles at the end of the scene.

Walt understands the circumstances of Thao's attempt at stealing the Gran Torino

Their developing friendship arrives at a new stage, when Walt needs help himself. He is unable to move a huge freezer out of the basement. Unusual for him, he rings at his neighbor's doorbell and asks for help. Quite symbolically, Thao takes the top in heaving up the freezer. After some argument, Walt accepts that he for once has to follow the young man's instructions. Despite their breathing hard, both make jokes about the situation and laugh which is another sign for their changed relationship. Although Walt wanted to sell the freezer for 60 dollars, he now gives it to his Hmong neighbors for 25.

Mutual help

In the following scene Thao can be seen at the back of Walt's house washing and waxing the Gran Torino he tried to steal earlier. Apart from the irony of the situation for him it is some sort of "justice". For Sue, however, this fits in with her idea of Walt being like a father to her brother:

> "It's nice of you to kind of look after him like this. He doesn't have any real role models in his life." (1:06:56)

Walt as a role model for Thao

Their own father was very traditional, probably educating Thao to live according to his Asian roots. Walt, on the other hand, though also "old school", shows Thao an "American" male lifestyle.

Becoming a male role model for Thao also implies that Walt asks him about his future plans. The hierarchical relation between "father" and "son" is expressed by Thao kneeling in the backyard with Walt towering above him. Low- and high-angle camera shots and reverse shots underline that idea, too. Thao thinks of going into sales. However, Walt tries to discourage him of that plan, mainly due to the fact that his son is a salesman for Japanese cars. He rather recommends him a job in a male-dominated field, such as construction, although he believes that he has "to man [Thao] up a little bit."

Thao's future plans

Learning to talk like a man	The first lesson Thao has to learn is to talk like a man. The best language coach Walt can think of is his Italian friend Martin whose behavior and attitude are of course sexually stereotyped, as the viewer sees him looking at some nude photographs in a men's magazine when Thao and Walt enter his shop. By exchanging their ordinary rude (but friendly) insults, Walt and Martin want to give Thao an example. However, when the Hmong teenager copies their speech, the barber pretends to be seriously annoyed and takes his gun to shoot him. Walt teaches him that he has to be friendly and polite to a stranger. To talk like a man, he should rather refer to male topics like his girlfriend, getting his car fixed or his boss's unjust behavior.
Successful training	Thao's progress can be seen when Walt takes him to a construction site. The veteran knows the superintendent of the site, the Irishman Tim Kennedy who should do him the favor of getting Thao a job. When Kennedy asks the Hmong teenager why he takes the bus instead of his own car, Thao complains about the owner of the garage as taught by Walt and Martin before:

> "My head gasket cracked. And the goddamned prick at the shop wants to bend me over for $2100." (1:14:42)

Thao gets a job in construction	The Irishman gives the Asian boy a job. On their way home Walt stops at a hardware store and equips Thao with some tools he thinks necessary for his new job. When Thao confesses that he lacks the money to pay for them, Walt tells him to pay his debt back on his first paycheck. In order to fix the deal, they shake hands.
Symbolic hand-shake	

Escalating Violence

> **INFO AT A GLANCE**
>
> **Retaliation and despair**
> - The Hmong gang waylays Thao to avenge his resistance against them. Smokie presses a lit cigarette into Thao's cheek.
> - When Walt notices the burn, he beats up the gangbanger, warning him to leave Thao alone.
> - In retaliation for this, the Hmong gang fires several shots in the direction of Thao's house.
> - Sue is brutally beaten and raped.
> - For obvious reasons, Walt feels guilty for the escalation.
> - In a conversation with Father Janovich he expresses his view that there will be no peace for Thao and Sue until the gang has gone away forever.

When Thao comes back home from work on one of the following days, he is waylaid by the Hmong gang. As before, the rap music is used as an alarming danger signal. When the five gangbangers encircle Thao, he has no chance to escape. While two or three of them are holding him firmly, the others grab some of his tools and destroy them. Finally, Smokie presses a lit cigarette into Thao's cheek as a revenge for his resistance. In the gang's logic they have to do something in retaliation for Thao's disobedience. For Smokie, it is a play on words, when he uses the phrase "save face" while injuring Thao.

Hmong gang-bangers take revenge in order to save face

Eastwood makes use of a hand-held camera with fast cuts in this scene. Close-ups reveal only details of the situation. By these means, the director increases the dramatic suspense. In particular, the extreme close-up of Smokie's face when he presses the cigarette into Thao's cheek makes him look more brutal, which is a prerequisite for Walt's later act of retaliation.

Hand-held camera and close-ups

A few days later when Thao bumps into the Korean War veteran, he tries to hide his face, because he does not want any further escalation. However, Walt notices his burn. Although the Hmong teenager does not give any details, Walt knows what has happened and asks for his cousin's address. Despite Thao's explicit wish not to do anything, the ex-soldier wants to set an example. He waits in his car in front of the gangbangers' house until his fellow gangbangers have left. Walt is in his "war-

Plot	
Walt in his "war-mode"	mode", indicated by the drum sounds in the background. Comparable to the gang's ambush on Thao, it is not a fair battle either, because he takes Smokie by surprise. In terms of brutality, Walt seems to be no better than Smokie. This is expressed by the low-angle camera position, which takes the point of view of the helpless Hmong who has to take the hard blows from above.
Physical exhaustion	When Walt comes back in the evening, he seems to feel his age as he is standing in front of his door shaking and grabbing for the knob. This should probably convey that he is not a tough soldier anymore but rather suffers from physical exhaustion. The next day scene, however, shows Walt's vitality again. He has invited Sue, Thao,
American barbecue	their mother and Youa for an American barbecue in his backyard. His jokes, e.g. about how his guests would like to have their dog steaks or that he wants to take out Youa, reveal that he is in a really good mood. In fact, it is the last moment all of them are having a great time. Walt is quite pleased to get to know that Thao asked Youa out. In order to allow Thao to do that in style, he
Walt lets Thao take his Gran Torino	lets him take his Gran Torino for the date. The teenager can hardly believe his luck.
Drive-by shooting	In sharp contrast to the joyful atmosphere at the barbecue party, the Hmong gangbangers strike back in one of the following nights. This is an essential part of the gang's logic to claim a higher prize for Walt's attack on Smokie. As a consequence, they fire several shots in the direction of Thao's house. But they deliberately aim high with their guns which can be seen from the bullet holes just below the ceiling.
Cinematographic elements to create suspense	Walt, who has been watching baseball on TV, gets out with his pistol, but the gangbangers have already left. Screaming from the neighbors' house, smoke and a continuous high (alarming) tone create a dramatic atmosphere. A hand-held camera follows the old man as he rushes into the neighbor's home. Inside there is panic, but nobody is seriously hurt. Only Thao is hit by a grazing shot at his neck. However, soon the family finds out that Sue is missing. Together with Walt, they have to wait for several hours before she comes home.

Hero to the Neighborhood

An alarming sound foreshadows that some catastrophe has happened. A close-up on Sue's blood-smeared face in the moment she enters the house makes clear what prize the family has to pay. Blood running down Sue's legs indicates that she has been raped. Whereas her family members cry and gather close to her, Walt stands apart. He is shocked and speechless at the development he himself set in motion. This is clearly shown by the glass that falls out of his hand and the close-ups of his painfully distorted face.

Sue has been beaten and raped

As he leaves the house, he can only say "No! No! No!" Inside his home, he wants to punish himself. Among other things, he smashes two glass windows of his cupboard, thus injuring his hands. Exhausted and destroyed he sits down in the dark, a metaphor for his inner troubles. Nick Schenk suggested in his script that Walt cries bitterly for the first time in fifty years, letting out all his frustration about his failed life, his family and the present situation. The director Eastwood obviously preferred the above-mentioned act of auto-aggression. However, one can see a tear rolling down Walt's cheek.

Walt feels guilty

Auto-aggression instead of tears

The old man is still sitting in his armchair, when later that night Father Janovich drops by. In contrast to previous conversations of the two of them this one gets quite personal. For the first time Walt seems to open his heart. He has obviously looked at old family photos which confirms the idea that he has been reflecting on his life. When Father Janovich tells him that the Hmong neighbors are too scared to tell anything to the police, Walt replies:

Father Janovich's late night visit

> "You know, Thao and Sue are never gonna find peace in this world as long as that gang's around. Until they go away, you know, forever." (1:27:15)

Being asked what he would do in Thao's place, the priest answers that he would probably take revenge "shoulder to shoulder with [Walt] and kill those guys." Although he himself would not tend to any act of violence, he seems to understand the involved logic of retaliation. Father Janovich seems to have learned a lot about life in the past weeks and months. His change becomes obvious

The priest understands the spiral of violence

Plot

Changed relationship

by the fact that he accepts Walt's offer of a beer which he had declined earlier on (in the bar). In fact, he takes four beers from the ice chest, two for each of them. At the end of the scene the quality of their relation seems to have changed, too. After having repetitively insisted on being called Mr. Kowalski, Walt now begs the priest to call him by his first name.

Walt's Death

INFO AT A GLANCE

Preparations for an anticlimax
- Thao cannot wait to avenge his sister's suffering, but Walt tells him to come back at 4 p.m.
- The old veteran prepares for his own death by e.g. having a haircut, a straight shave and a fitted suit for his funeral.
- Walt locks up Thao to prevent him from becoming a murderer.
- He makes two confessions: He tells the Hmong teenager that he was awarded with a Silver Star medal, although he killed an innocent Korean boy. His formal confession to Father Janovich gives the priest a hint of what might happen within the next few hours. Therefore he calls the police.
- Walt provokes the Hmong gangbangers in front of their house. When he tries to get out his lighter, the gang shoots him down, as expected. For Walt, his death is a redemption of all the evil in his life. He didn't' even have a gun on him.
- The gangbangers are arrested. As a lot of people witnessed their shooting an unarmed man, they will be imprisoned for the rest of their lives.
- Thao inherits the Gran Torino.

Thao has to wait for his revenge

In the morning of the following day Thao cannot wait to avenge his sister's suffering. Walt presumably has been thinking all night about a plan that the gang "won't have a chance", as he said to Father Janovich. He has come up with something he does not tell his Hmong friend. He only advises him to calm down, not to make any mistake and come back at 4 p.m. The whole scene is full of aggression and emotional depth. Thus it is no surprise that it is dominated by close-up shots of Walt's and Thao's faces.

As Walt is prepared "to finish things", he wants to bring his matters in order. The audience witnesses him mowing his lawn for the last time, before he is having a bath. For the first time in his life he allows himself to have a cigarette inside the house. Other preparations are connected with his planned funeral. Not only does he have a final haircut, he also asks his friend Martin for a straight shave for the first time ever. He seems to be very concerned about his outward appearance because in the following scene we see Walt having a fitted suit specially made for him in a tailor's store.

Walt's concern for his own appearance at his funeral

Last but not least, he goes to confession to Father Janovich. The priest is rather shocked about seeing Walt in his church, expecting him to have committed a serious crime, such as killing the Hmong gangbangers. However, the veteran does not confess anything except for kissing another woman at a Christmas party back in 1968. He also admits having evaded to pay his taxes for once which seems to him "the same as stealing". The thing which seems to have bothered him for most of his life are his family relations:

Strange confession to Father Janovich

> "Oh, lastly, I was never very close with my two sons. I don't know them. I didn't know how." (1:33:37)

Quite symbolically, some sort of lattice inside the confessional booth separates him from Father Janovich. As the priest realizes that Walt's words don't add up to a full confession, he asks him directly whether he is going to do something in retaliation for what happened to Sue. Walt does not reply anything. When the priest wishes him to go in peace, the old man turns around and confirms: "I am at peace."

Walt is "at peace"

A second confession follows when Thao returns just before 4 p.m. Walt carefully reassembles his 30-06 M1 Garand Rifle and his colt he just cleaned and oiled. By this, he makes Thao believe that there will be a violent showdown, although he has planned the contrary. He tricks him into going to the basement to show him his Silver Star medal. There the young Hmong asks Walt how many men he killed in Korea and how it is like to kill somebody.

Signals for a violent resolution

The veteran admits that he shot 13 or more men. While Thao should close the box with Walt's memories, the old man goes upstairs and locks him in. Parallel to the

Second confession

former confession in church the latticed basement door separates Walt from Thao when he confesses:

> "You wanna know what it's like to kill a man? Well, it's goddamn awful, that's what it is. The only thing worse is getting a medal of honor for killing some poor kid that wanted to just give up, that's all. Yeah, some scared little gook just like you. I shot him right in the face with that rifle you were holding in there a while ago. Not a day goes by that I don't think about it … and you don't want that on your soul. Now, I got blood on my hands. I'm soiled. That's why I'm going it alone tonight." (1:36:33)

Important function of the camera

In this second confession Walt is towering above Thao which symbolizes his dominance in this specific moment. Close-ups of his face show his inner turmoil. Interestingly, he calls the teenager a "friend" who he does not want to waste his life. Before he finally leaves, he hands over his dog to Phong. They do not understand each other, but the old Hmong woman does not protest when the white man leaves Daisy with her.

Father Janovich has called the police

Some time later Walt phones Sue from the Veteran's bar phone booth and orders her to free Thao from his house. Meanwhile Father Janovich has been waiting for hours with two policemen in front of the gangbangers' house. Obviously the priest interpreted Walt's remarks in the right way. However, as there is no proven or visible threat, the policemen do not want to wait any longer. They force the priest to leave with them.

The circumstances of Walt's death come as a surprise for the audience. With Clint Eastwood's reputation a final shootout in which he kills the gangsters is probably expected by most viewers. The short sequence of scenes in which he prepares his self-sacrifice might be confusing or mystifying, but in the dramatic pace at the end these scenes are easily overlooked.

Provoking a showdown

The veteran waits until dusk falls when he finally confronts the gangbangers. With the camera behind Walt, the audience starts watching the scene from his point of view. Walt keeps on insulting the gang members with his racist slurs in order to provoke some reaction.

Spider is the first to point a gun at him, while the others are standing in front of the house, waiting for a showdown to come. The noisy confrontation draws the attention of the Hmong neighbors who come out of their houses or look out of their windows. Their witnessing the following events is important, because the gangbangers' imprisonment will be based on their testimony.

Witnesses

When the veteran pulls out a cigarette, the gangbangers become nervous and pull their weapons without firing. Walt, on the other hand, has come unarmed. As in other scenes before, he forms an imaginary gun with his hand and pretends to pull the trigger. Drum sounds announce that the situation might reach the most important result.

Drum sounds announce Walt's death

Finally, Walt asks the gangbangers whether they have got a light (for his cigarette). He answers the rhetorical question himself with: "No. Me. I've got light." Obviously, this has a double meaning. Literally, it refers to the fact that he is about to take his old Zippo lighter out of his pocket which he has kept since the Korean War and which has always been a reminder of his shameful deeds 50 years ago. On the other hand, his remark has a figurative meaning, as he is going to bring light into the Hmong's crimes. Quite deliberately, he makes a move as if he is going to pull a gun. To prevent this, all gang-bangers simultaneously shoot at him.

The lighter

To emphasize the dramatic moment, the camera focuses on Walt's body hit by uncountable bullets. Finally, the music stops and the old man falls down in slow motion and in absolute silence. When his body hits the ground, there is a noise again. An extreme close-up of his old lighter makes sure that he came unarmed. With his arms stretched out on the ground, the dead body – seen from above – looks like a Christ figure or cross. It is a visualization of Walt's salvation, his final successful attempt to come to terms with his personal guilt from the Korean War. The emotional impact of that moment is supported by the melancholy title song setting in. Blended over the high-angle shot of the corpse, lights of police cars appear, indicating that the authorities have

Dramatic anticlimax

The outstretched arms as a visualization of Walt's salvation

Putting the gang-bangers under arrest

been called immediately. Thao and Sue arrive in Walt's Gran Torino. Their facial expressions show that they fear the worst. Though officially not allowed, a Hmong police officer tells them what happened. Close-ups of Father Janovich and Sue reveal that they are completely shocked. Tears roll down Sue's cheeks. Thao seems to be torn between sorrow for Walt and hatred for his cousin and the gang. With regard to them, the camera focuses on Spider and Smokie, the two leaders, who are directed to two different squad cars.

Sue's and Thao's reaction

With the ongoing music of the song "Gran Torino", the scene changes to the day of Walt's funeral. Thao and Sue have put on their traditional dresses for the ceremony. They are seated on one side of the church, while Walt's family sits on the other. Mitch, his oldest son, is obviously surprised by the presence of the Asian neighbors. The dead Walt, laid out in a coffin, is wearing his new fitted suit. Father Janovich takes up the topic of life and death again. However, this time he admits that he knew nothing about life and death before he met Walt.

Walt's funeral

The audience is only presented the beginning of the eulogy. Soon there is a clear cut to the opening of Walt's last will. Whereas all of his family is seated in the middle of the law office, Thao remains standing in a corner, indicating that he is of less significance for the legal procedure and probably the least likely to get anything from the deceased. To the nasty surprise of his family, Walt gives his house to the church, which is probably a result of his changed relation with Father Janovich. It gets even worse for Ashley, when she comes to know that the 1972 Gran Torino goes to Walt's "friend" Thao. A pause made by the lawyer as well as the granddaughter's hopeful smile before the announcement emphasize the unexpected turn of events.

Walt's last will

In contrast to Ashley's wishes, Thao inherits the Gran Torino

Unable to believe his luck, the Hmong teenager seems to find it hard to suppress a smile. When the piano sets in for the final song "Gran Torino", sung by Clint Eastwood himself, Thao's picture in the law office dissolves into one showing him in his own car together with Daisy on the front-passenger seat. He is driving alongside Lake St. Clair. In a deeper, figurative sense this may be interpreted as a change from a teenager to a grown-up man.

Dissolve emphasizes a change in status

② Analysis and Interpretation

Narrative Structure

> **INFO AT A GLANCE**
>
> **A Hollywood drama**
> - Despite its complex sign system, the movie *Gran Torino* can be interpreted as a text with a narrative structure.
> - With its clear sequence of the introduction of the situation, its disruption and resolution, *Gran Torino* strongly fits in with the drama genre.
> - The linear story is told through Walt Kowalski's eyes.
> - The plot focuses on Walt's development and his friendship to Thao and his family. One major subplot, however, is the veteran's relation to Father Janovich.
> - Suspense culminates in chapter 28. The viewers' expectations of a showdown as a resolution of the conflict are contradicted, as the movie ends in the anticlimax of Walt's death.
> - Two funerals frame the plot.

Analyzing a movie is by no means different to a closer analysis of a novel or a drama. Despite the complex sign system of camera movements, lighting, sound and symbols, the interpretation of the narrative structure can be boiled down to looking for genre patterns, points of view, plot and subplots.

Gran Torino is a typical Hollywood drama, a genre which focuses on inner conflicts. Plots often include strained family relations, tragic developments and emotional problems. Usually protagonists are able to solve their difficulties by brave actions. As far as structure is concerned, dramas follow the pattern of a certain situation, its disruption and resolution. All this is true for *Gran Torino* as well:

Specific situation, disruption and resolution

> "The situation is of the widowed life of racist Walt, the disruption is the introduction of the gang and this resolves itself by the gang being defeated but also by Walt's racism being resolved also." (https://chadwickfilm.wordpress.com/2010/01/31/what-message-does-gran-torino-convey)

The movie sets out with the problem of Walt's racist attitude and unfolds his hidden bad conscience. Only later is Thao's conflict added. As in a drama everything has a clear-cut narrative resolution, the ending covers both problems at once. By his self-sacrifice the Korean War veteran overcomes his racial prejudices and makes sure that the Hmong gang is sent to prison for the rest of their lives.

The narrative is very simple, as the plot unfolds in a linear way. There are no flashbacks which disrupt the sequence of events although Walt's past plays a central role. It is revealed in bits and pieces by the information the protagonist gives himself. The audience is not confronted with shocking pictures of Korean warfare (except a small photo in Walt's box). The whole story is told through the eyes of Walt Kowalski, whose fate links all characters of the movie. Certainly, the events center around the protagonist's slow change from a grumpy, racially prejudiced old man to a likeable character due to his friendship with his Hmong neighbors. In particular Walt's relation to Thao who he takes under his wing to help him to become a man is the most prominent storyline.

Linear plot

The story is told through Walt's eyes

However, there are at least two subplots in *Gran Torino*. On the one hand, there is Walt's difficult relationship to his two sons, daughters-in-law and his grandchildren. Although he has two sons, the movie focuses on Mitch, Walt's eldest son whose story is presumably representative for both of them. That both sons are rather distanced to their father is shown in the opening scene at Dorothy Kowalski's funeral. Walt's problems with the grandchildren generation is presented by his relation to Ashley.

Subplot 1: Walt's family problems

On the other hand, there is the subplot of the old protagonist and young Father Janovich. At first Walt is quite reserved towards the priest's wish of making him confess his sins. But in the course of the movie both open their hearts and due to the veteran's revelation of his haunted mind, Father Janovich learns a lot about life and death.

Subplot 2: Walt and Father Janovich

One might say that the film starts as a comedy. In particular, Walt's racist comments were met with big laughs by most American audiences. However, soon the

Comedy and suspense

Analysis and Interpretation

gang conflict adds suspense to the plot. Important stages are Thao's initiation ritual and the gangbangers' return when they try to make the teenager join them by force. At this instance the old veteran scares away the Hmong gangbangers by warning them to get off his lawn. In one of the following scenes Walt saves Sue from harassment by African American youngsters. The arc of suspense culminates in the drive-by shooting and Sue's return. For obvious reasons, it is not shown what happened to her. Her blood-smeared face and body and the reactions of her family are enough to visualize her pain.

Expectations of the audience

The anticlimax when Walt finally confronts the gang comes as a surprise. Clint Eastwood's former roles as some lonesome shooter as well as Hollywood film traditions trigger the expectation of a violent showdown. *Gran Torino* itself enhances this idea by the suggestion of Walt's atrocities in the Korean War and the intrinsic logic of retaliation. Certain incidents, however, hint at an unexpected ending. Walt's horoscope on his birthday, for example, literally refers to an "anticlimax". Additionally, the protagonist's frequent forming an imaginary gun with his fingers foreshadows his final abandonment of taking a weapon with him. Worth mentioning in the context of the overall structure is also the fact that the movie starts and ends with a funeral. The church ceremonies for Dorothy and Walt build a frame for the presented conflicts and Thao's development.

Foreshadowing

Two funerals frame the plot

Setting

INFO AT A GLANCE

Highland Park – a troubled spot in Motor City Detroit
- *Gran Torino* is set in Highland Park, Michigan, which belongs to the Metropolitan area of Detroit.
- Throughout its history, the city has been connected with the local factories of Ford, Chrysler and General Motors.
- Metropolitan Detroit was particularly hit by the 2008 financial crisis, in the middle of which the movie was released.
- Once a booming city, Highland Park is now part of "that industrial graveyard called Detroit" (Dargis 2008).

Nick Schenk suggested in his screenplay to set the movie in Minneapolis, after he himself had worked at a local Ford plant, side by side with several Korean War veterans with racial prejudices against Asians. He had also got to know Hmong immigrants there, so that his own experience has predetermined the constellation of characters in the film. However, Clint Eastwood obviously had the idea that Walt Kowalski's lifelong work at Ford corresponds better to Motor City Detroit. Although the scenes were shot in locations like Royal Oak, Warren and Grosse Pointe Park, all within Metro Detroit, Highland Park was chosen to be the area where Walt and Thao live.

Nick Schenk's personal experiences

At the beginning of the 20th century, Highland Park quickly developed from a small village into an industrial landmark. The Highland Park Ford Plant became the flagship factory of Ford in 1913, when the first assembly line was introduced there. Henry Ford offered the highest average living standard for workers in the U.S. Moreover, in 1925 Chrysler Corporation was founded close to it, establishing its headquarters in Highland Park for the next 70 years. Not surprisingly, the population rapidly grew until the late 1930s. However, Ford began to wind down its operations in the 1950s and closed its plant in 1973, although the company remained in the Detroit area. There was another major loss of industrial jobs when Chrysler moved to Auburn Hills in 1992.

Rise of Highland Park

Above all, the 2008 financial crisis hit the Metropolitan Detroit area severely. Two of the "Big Three" (General Motors and Chrysler) were forced into bankruptcy and had to be bailed out by the Obama Administration. In 2009, Highland Park was a

2008 financial crisis

> "site of some of the worst poverty in the states. Setting the film in the context of the auto industry is not coincidental, and the fate of Kowalski's character and his dying (or, at the very least, seriously troubled) industry are intertwined. Both appear to be on their way out, but the cherry perfect condition of the Gran Torino speaks of a past, muscular glory." (www.racismreview.com/blog/2009/01/17/gran-torino-white-masculinity-racism)

Analysis and Interpretation

Pictures of decline	*Gran Torino* shows various pictures of this decline, although the houses next to Walt's perfectly kept home were artificially put in a rather bad shape, as production designer Rob Lorenz explains, in order to show the people's poverty and despair. One of the most depressing settings is used in the scene with the three African Americans. Obviously, people have put rubbish next to the fence, and the whole area looks run-down. Thao's encounters with the Hmong gangbangers take also place amidst several areas of decay, e.g. when he bumps into the Latino gang and his Hmong cousin.
White flight	The severe economic problems described above have led to a steady decline of inhabitants and a change in population structure. White flight began in the late 1950s and accelerated after the 1967 Detroit 12th Street Riot. Instead, mainly African Americans moved into Highland Park. This is the situation in which Walt Kowalski finds himself in *Gran Torino*. When he went there some time after the Korean War (1950–1053), it used to be an all-white neighborhood, consisting of lower middle-class people who more or less knew each other as they all were connected to the automobile industry. At the beginning of the 21st century he is the only white person left – except for the woman who lives opposite him. Statistics confirm his personal experience. According to the United States Census Bureau only 5.85% of the population in Highland Park is white.
Gran Torino does not reflect the real racial makeup of Detroit	However, Eastwood's fictionalized neighborhood stands in sharp contrast to the overall racial makeup of Highland Park, because there live only 0.16% Asian immigrants. With over 90% the vast majority of the people there are African Americans. Many of these cannot find a job. According to the data of the United
Poverty and unemployment	States Census Bureau, 15.6% of the population in Highland Park is unemployed, which is much more than the national rate of 5.8%. The rate of people living below the poverty line in the area is 205% higher than the national average. Economic problems, hopelessness and people's ambiguity of belonging are the well-known base for criminal activities.

The table below shows not only the reported number of crimes, but also the amount of crimes committed per 100,000 people. According to this table, the overall crime rate is 74% higher than the national average. When it comes to violent crimes, Highland Park has a rate that is 297% higher than the Michigan average. The risk of being a victim to a crime is 1 in 21. Thus it can be argued that the attempted theft of the Gran Torino, Sue's rape and the gangbangers' shooting of Walt are by no means unlikely, but rather reflect the infamous crime rate of the area.

Highland Park's high crime rate

Reported Annual Crime in Highland Park (2015)

	Reported incidents	Highland Park/ 100k people	Michigan/ 100k people	National/ 100k people
Total crime	501	4,973	2,301	2,860
Murder	5	49.6	5.8	4.9
Rape	9	89.3	65.0	38.6
Robbery	47	466.5	78.6	101.9
Assault	105	1,042.3	266.2	237.8
Violent Crime	166	1,648	416	373
Burglary	65	645.2	403.5	491.4
Theft	197	1,955.5	1,323.2	1,775.4
Vehicle Theft	73	724.6	158.9	220.2
Property Crimes	335	3,325	1,886	2,487

http://www.areavibes.com/highland+park-mi/crime (8 April 2017)

Analysis and Interpretation

Characters

Walt Kowalski

> **INFO AT A GLANCE**
>
> **A racist who turns out to have a good heart**
> - With respect to his values, Walt is "still living in the '50s."
> - His conservatism, patriotism and racial prejudices make him a typical white American of that generation.
> - He worked at Ford for his entire life.
> - He is haunted by his Korean War experiences, in particular by his killing innocent people.
> - In Walt's racist worldview, he does not distinguish between different Asian ethnic groups. For him, they are all alike. Thus his Hmong neighbors remind him of his bad conscience.
> - With his 78 years, he is, so to speak, an outdated old timer like his vintage car, the Gran Torino, alienated from the changing world around him.
> - He is also alienated from his two sons and their families and portrayed as a grumpy loner.
> - His behavior is stereotypically masculine, e.g. solving problems on his own, protecting or defending himself and others with a gun and not going to the doctors.
> - He becomes a male role model for Thao.
> - Walt's getting into touch with his Hmong neighbors changes him. He has to learn that he has got more in common with his Hmong neighbors than with his own family.
> - Walt realizes that he is responsible for the escalation of violence.
> - Sacrificing himself in the confrontation with the Hmong gangbangers, he finally finds peace as he takes the chance to atone for his lifelong guilt.

Modeled on Stanley Kowalski

Walt Kowalski is probably modeled on Tennessee Williams's protagonist Stanley Kowalski in his play *A Streetcar Named Desire*. Like Walt, Stanley is a Polish immigrant and a car plant worker, lives in a "broken world" and tends to use violence instead of words. He has a friend called Mitch, which is the name of Walt Kowalski's eldest son. The allusion to Williams's play also emphasizes the fact that *Gran Torino* has to be seen in the tradition of psychological realism in American drama.

Walt is still "living in the '50s"

In one of the very first sentences Walt Kowalski is described by his son as still living "in the '50s". This characterization is definitely true for his values and conceptions. Despite the great inner distance to his sons and grandchildren, traditional family bonds are important to him, in particular in the present situation where he has just lost his wife. Although he went to church mainly for Dorothy's sake, he expects his family to come to the funeral, to dress and behave respectfully which obviously cannot be taken for granted if you look at Ashley's generation.

Traditional values: family and Church

Having grown up during the Second World, having fought for his country in Korea and the Cold War experience have shaped Walt's deeply rooted patriotism. He is the only one in the movie who has got an American flag hanging outside his house (see picture below).

Patriotism

Analysis and Interpretation

Hatred of Toyota	Walt's patriotism is also influenced by his working at Ford. He cannot understand his son's choice of a Japanese Toyota, from the largest car producer in the world which stands in global competition with the Detroit "Big Three". Quite often he seems to have complained to his son Mitch that he did not support the American economy by buying a "rice-burner".
Concept of white predominance	His conservative conception of society in general is that of a white predominance. Therefore he once moved to Highland Park, in former times an all-white middle-class neighborhood. For decades he used to live next to people with the same ethnic and cultural background, mutually confirming each other's values, e.g. keeping their property in a perfect shape.
Racial prejudices	Now he is almost the only white American left. Fed by racial prejudices, he looks down on anyone who is different in race, cultural practice or religious belief. Most obviously, this can be seen by his racial slurs with which he expresses his contempt for his Hmong neighbors. The ritual slaughtering of a cock in the course of the birth ceremony is commented by him as barbaric. His addressing the African American young men as "spooks" also belongs into that context.
Prejudices are reiterated in jokes	The only friends (except for the Italian barber) he seems to have are his old war buddies who he meets at a bar. Their old prejudices are reiterated over and over again which can be seen by the following joke told by Walt himself:

> "There's a Mexican, a Jew and a colored guy go into a bar.
> The bartender looks up and says: 'Get the fuck out of here.'"
> (17:26)

Old-fashioned taste	That Walt hangs on to the past can additionally be observed from his taste. The Pabst Blue Ribbon beer is a classic, rather old-fashioned brand which peaked in the 1970s. Although Asian food is quite popular in the U.S.A. nowadays, Walt is not familiar with it. In all his beliefs, conceptions and preferences he is by no means an exception, but rather a typical representative of his generation.

The most important experience in his whole life was fighting in the Korean War. Beyond doubt, on the one hand the majority of his racial prejudices is derived from this time. On the other hand, his personal experiences may be the reason for his tendency to solve certain problems with his rifle which he brought home after the war. Last but not least, they are the source of his unhappiness because he has never come to terms with what he did during the war. Walt learnt to wear a mask, hiding the pictures of cruelties on both sides and blocking out the memory of his own guilt. When asked by Thao, he admits that he shot at least 13 people. However, what has haunted him his whole life is what he did without being ordered to do so:

Consequences of the Korean War

> "You wanna know what it's like to kill a man? Well, it's goddamn awful, that's what it is. They only thing worse is getting a medal of honor for killing some poor kid that wanted to just give up, that's all. Yeah, some scared little gook just like you. I shot him right in the face with that rifle you were holding in there a while ago. Not a day goes by that I don't think about it […]." (1:36:33)

Haunted by shooting an innocent teenager

His bad conscience has prevented him from finding peace with himself. His Hmong neighbors remind him of his horrible deeds as they look like the Korean people to him. He is unable to distinguish between Koreans, Chinese, Japanese or Hmong. For him (as for most Americans) they all look the same.

Hmong neighbors remind Walt of his war crimes

Walt Kowalski went to Korea in 1950 when he was twenty years old. The movie *Gran Torino* is set in 2008, so that he is about 78, the same age as his actor Clint Eastwood. Amongst the Hmong community which gradually replaced the white inhabitants of Highland Park, he looks like an old timer, unable to understand the changes around him. Like his vintage car, the 1972 Ford Gran Torino, he seems to be out of place. Maybe that is one of the reasons that there is such a strong connection between the two. While working at Ford Walt put the steering column in this car, but there is more behind it. Although he seems not to drive the car any more, he cares for it like a father for his child.

Walt as an outdated old timer

Analysis and Interpretation

Maintaining his property as his "last defense against change"

Polishing and waxing the Ford seems to be one of the few pleasures left in his life. Like his car which is in mint condition, Walt's house sticks out of the other ones in the run-down neighborhood, as it is perfectly kept. It is "his castle, his fortress. Maintaining this property, like maintaining his car, is his last defense against change" (www.ethicsdaily.com/gran-torino-cms-13602).

Walt and his familiy

Given all these factors, it is no surprise that Walt is presented as a grumpy and lonely man from the very beginning. Not only at the funeral and the following feast he seems to be completely alienated from his two sons who are fed up with quarreling with him. Mitch and his father phone each other only once in a while, but Walt never tells his family what really bothers him. He even conceals his fatal lung cancer after Mitch told him that he is busy with some bills. That they do not really know each other gets most obvious on Walt's birthday when Mitch's and Karen's presents indicate that they think he is somewhat restricted in his physical abilities.

Walt suffers from the fact that he has not been able to keep close contact to his sons. In his confession to Father Janovich he feels guilty about his failed family relationships:

> "Oh, lastly, I was never very close with my two sons. I don't know them. I didn't know how." (1:33:37)

Loneliness

So he spends most of his time alone sitting on his porch, reading, overlooking the street or drinking beer. Until the moment Sue shows him a way to change his solitary daily routine by inviting him to come to their party, his only companion is his dog Daisy.

Stereotypical gender concepts

Walt's general behavior is stereotypically masculine so that he is a perfect role model for Thao. As stated above, he does not show his troubled mind but has learnt to wear a mask to conceal his feelings. He is not only good at maintaining cars, but is able to do all sorts of chores. With its enormous horsepower, the Gran Torino is called a "muscle car" which underlines stereotypical features of a male identity. Walt's hand-operated lawn-mower emphasizes the same idea. Moreover, his selection of tools in the garage does not only surprise Thao, but would make any man envious. Furthermore, men are said not to go to the doctors, which is also true for Walt. Despite his age and his frequent coughing up blood, his last visit to his regular doctor must have been a long time ago which the viewer gets to know by the fact that Dr. Feldman retired three years ago.

Walt is used to solving his problems on his own which can be seen in various episodes of the movie. He does not accept help from his son or granddaughter but rather prefers getting the chairs from the basement alone. The same applies to the scene in which he tries to get the heavy freezer up from the basement. And lastly he decides to deal with the Hmong gang on his own and does not call the police, as Father Janovich advises him to do.

Solving problems alone

Moreover, his strategy of solving conflicts is to use force. The first thing which comes to his mind when he notices that someone is going to steal his car, is not calling the police but taking out his gun. When the fighting between the Hmong gangbangers and Thao's family spills over to his lawn, he is reminded of the war situation decades ago. Therefore he takes the rifle he brought home from Korea to scare away Spider and his friends. Later he brutally beats up Smokie in retaliation of his burning a cigarette into Thao's cheek. Last but not least, Walt's self-sacrifice involves a violent showdown.

Use of violence

With respect to his beliefs and conceptions, Walt seems to be rather stubborn. For quite a while he is presented as a racially prejudiced man, always grumbling about his Asian neighbors. Only unwillingly, he becomes a hero to the neighborhood when he saves Thao and later Sue. The ice breaks on his birthday, offering him "second chances" in his life, as his horoscope foreshadowed. Quite important for Walt's liking of Thao is the little episode with the white woman living opposite. When she drops her groceries, some teenagers who are passing by make fun of her. Thao, on the other hand, helps her instantly.

"Second chances" come on Walt's birthday

The groceries' episode

Analysis and Interpretation

Walt's ambiguity of belonging

Invited by Sue, Walt enjoys the food and the company of the Hmong people. After the shaman's precise analysis of his psyche, the veteran observes the respectful treatment of the older people which he misses in his own family. He realizes that he and the Hmong share a conservative belief in sticking to one's own country and its traditions. The painful question arises in him as to where he really belongs. Looking at himself in the mirror, he has to recognize an inconvenient truth:

> "God, I've got more in common with these gooks than I do my own spoilt rotten family. Jesus Christ. Happy birthday!" (46:15)

Metaphorical self-reflection

The self-reflection in the mirror is quite metaphorical. Beyond doubt, it is a turning-point in his life. It is also the starting-point of his taking Thao under his wing. On that very day he advises the teenager how to deal with women, shortly after he criticized him for letting Youa go. A little later Walt teaches him to talk like a man und

Male role model

provides him with a job. He becomes the male role model Thao never had before, and he more and more befriends the youngster and his sister Sue. So in the course of the movie the Hmong neighbors become

The Hmong neighbors as family substitute

Walt's family substitute. With them – not with his own relatives – he has a barbecue party in his backyard.

Walt's responsibility for the spiral of violence

When Sue is beaten and raped, Walt is completely shattered. This is not only due to the emotional bonds he has developed, but above all because he knows that he is responsible for the spiral of violence. He was the one to first beat up Smokie who in return claimed a higher prize. As a consequence, Walt punishes himself by hitting his fist into the cupboard. In one of the rare moments in which he shows his feelings, one can see a tear rolling down his cheek.

Finally "at peace"

However, in the night after the Catholic priest has left him, he goes through all possible alternatives. When Thao drops by the next morning, Walt has come to a decision. One can assume a mixture of several motifs. Most importantly, he wants to pay for all the horrible things in his past by sacrificing himself. In the confessions to Father Janovich and Thao he opens his heart, admitting that he has found a way to be "at peace". When the bullets of the gangbangers finally hit him, he is redeemed from his sins. His salvation is symbolized by the cross he forms with his arms when he lies dead on the ground.

Obviously, Walt's self-sacrifice is also a way to avoid a long and painful suffering to death from his lung cancer. He is definitely not a man who wants to see his physical strength decreasing and have to rely on others. The strong symbolic signs at the end, however, give the audience the impression that this motif seems less important. What counts more is the fact that Walt's death opens the way to restore law and order in the neighborhood, as the gangbangers are put to jail.

Analysis and Interpretation

Thao and the Hmong Community
(Sue, Phong, Smokie and Spider)

> **INFO AT A GLANCE**
>
> **"The girls go to college, and the boys go to jail"**
> - The Hmong are a forgotten people, scattered over Laos, Thailand and Vietnam. They fought for the Americans in the Vietnam War after which they had to go into U.S. exile.
> - Most Hmong girls are able to adapt to American society, while the boys do not accept their fathers' values. Having no orientation, some of them get criminal.
> - Thao Vang Lor, a 16-year-old teenager, grows up in a female-dominated house without any male role model.
> - He lacks self-confidence. Torn between gender roles, Hmong traditions and American standards of living, he does not know where he belongs to and searches for an identity.
> - Easy to push around, he is pressurized into joining the Hmong gang. After his initiation ritual of stealing the Gran Torino failed, he wants to keep a distance, so the gangbangers try to take him by force.
> - As compensation for his attempted theft Thao has to do odd jobs for Walt Kowalski. For the first time in his life he really rises to the tasks presented to him.
> - Being taught to talk and behave like a man, he grows from a teenager into a male adult.
> - He first accepts the gangbangers' brutality and does not want Walt to do anything against it. Only after Sue's rape he is willing to kill them. However, he is locked up in the basement of Walt's house, because Walt wants to prevent him from getting blood on his hands.
> - To his own surprise, he inherits Walt's Gran Torino, giving him the opportunity to assimilate into American society.
> - Sue is a strong young woman, able to live in both worlds of Hmong tradition and modern western liberalism. One sign for this is that she has a white boyfriend.
> - Due to her self-confidence she does not shy away from any open confrontation with the Hmong gang or the African American men.
> - Sue bridges the gap between her family and Walt Kowalski. Without her, they would not have become friends.
> - Her grandmother Phong is a first-generation immigrant, full of prejudices against white America. She does not speak English.
> - Spider (Sue's and Thao's cousin), Smokie and the other Hmong gangbangers terrorize the neighborhood. There is no resistance against them within the community. People do not dare to talk to the police.
> - The peer group follows its own rules of enforcing their status by violence and retaliation.
> - Being witnessed when shooting the unarmed Walt, they are arrested.

The Hmong people are unknown to most Americans which is reflected by Walt's question to Sue where Hmong should be. Hoping that the movie *Gran Torino* would make Americans aware of this forgotten ethnic group, there was a widespread support in the U.S. Hmong community. As explained by Sue on their ride home in Walt's truck, the Hmong were scattered over Laos, Thailand and Vietnam. Their unfortunate fate was that they fought on the American side in the Vietnam War (1955–1975). After the Communist turnover tens of thousands of Hmong were persecuted and killed by the new rulers. Naturally, those who were allowed went into U.S. exile in the first immigration wave (1975–1976). Primarily, Hmong soldiers were evacuated or given asylum. Due to the Refugee Act of 1980, the families of these men were permitted to enter the U.S. Indicated by their surname, the Lor family (Thao's grandmother and mother) must have come to the States in this second wave of immigration.

> Forgotten ethnic group

> Persecuted for their participation in the Vietnam War

> Lor family came in the second wave of immigration

Today the Hmong are spread all over the country, mainly in California, Minnesota and Wisconsin. Michigan, however, in which the movie is set, is reported to have only about 6000 Hmong people. According to the 2010 Census, 260,000 people of Hmong descent live in the U.S. Current issues of the Hmong minority such as education, poverty, gang violence and race relations are well portrayed in *Gran Torino*. Due to the fact that they were hill-farmers, many first-generation immigrants in the Hmong community lack formal education. Additionally, according to government statistics, 40% of Hmong Americans drop out of school (2013). As a consequence, they have difficulties in finding a job and are exposed to poverty. About a third of all Hmong families in the U.S. live under the poverty line.

> American Hmong today: poverty, unemployment, gang violence

It is a well-known fact in the Hmong community that their girls find it easier to adapt to the American way of life. Sue sums it up with the words:

> Hmong girls fit in better

> It's really common. Hmong girls over here fit in better. The girls go to college, and the boys go to jail." (36:39)

Analysis and Interpretation

Background information in Schenk's script

Nick Schenk's explanation for that phenomenon is given in a part of his script which was not taken up by the director Eastwood:

> Sue
> Hmong girls slip in and out of the culture more easily. Date who we want, stay close to other mothers, but are able to keep a foot on each side of the fence. The boys fall through the cracks.
>
> Walt
> Why?
>
> Sue
> It's tough. The boys float around. The fathers belong in a totally different world and the boys have no one to turn to. Does that make sense?
>
> Walt
> Not sure. No.
>
> Sue
> The boys don't ask their fathers for advice, because over here, their fathers no longer have the answers.
> Hmong boys become almost invisible, they end up banding together and it all goes to hell from there.
> (http://www.imsdb.com/scripts/Gran-Torino.html; p. 81)

Thao

Thao's father

The Hmong community presented in *Gran Torino* seems to illustrate these facts in a perfect way. First of all, there is the 16-year-old Thao Vang Lor. He has grown up in a female-dominated house with his grandmother Phong, his mother Vu and his sister Sue. The audience does not get to know anything about the whereabouts of the missing husbands. During the festivities there are some men to be seen, but the relations between all of them remain unclear. The only thing we get to know is that Thao's father was very traditional. Sue's description of him being "hard" and "really old school" suggests that he educated them according to Hmong values, e.g. to be obedient, but failed in teaching them to adapt to American society.

Torn apart between different gender roles and national identities

The probably fatherless boy is torn apart between different gender roles and national identities. At home he is expected to do the washing-up, an activity with which he is introduced right before the birth ceremony at the beginning of the movie. In Schenk's script, Thao's grandmother Phong denies his male identity altogether by saying: "Thao is not a man." In the movie her Hmong words are subtitled as follows:

"Thao is not a man"

> "Look at him washing dishes. He does whatever his sister orders him to do. How could he ever become the man of the house?" (10:00)

To underline this, one can see an elderly man putting more dishes into the sink. For the Hmong man, Thao almost seems to be invisible as he does not acknowledge his presence.

Throughout the first half of the movie Thao's male identity is questioned. The Latino gang asks him whether he is a "boy or a girl." On his first visit to Thao's house Smokie comments on his doing yard work "like a woman". Most obvious is Walt's repetitive attributing him with female derogative phrases like "pussy". Moreover, the veteran complains that he has got "no balls", meaning he is at everyone's beck and call.

Questioning Thao's male identity

On the other hand, Thao is rather dubious about his national or cultural identity. Born in the United States he is American, but he cannot deny his Asian roots. At the beginning of the movie he lacks everything which is generally accepted to be part of an ideal (white) American man: a job, a (white) girlfriend and a car. However, he does not take part in the shaman's birth ceremony like everybody else, either. Having washed the dishes, he leaves secretly.

Ambigious cultural identity

Due to his ambiguity of belonging, Thao "doesn't know which direction to go in", as Sue explains to Walt. This corresponds to his lack of self-confidence. Easy to push around as he is, he cannot resist Spider's 'offer' to join the gang. However, when the initiation ritual fails and he nearly gets shot by Walt, his wish for independence awakens again. He resists being carried away by the gangbangers, but without Walt's interference he would have ended in their custody.

Lacking self-confidence, Thao is easy to push around

On account of his shame for having tried to steal the Gran Torino, it takes a while before he tells his family about it. Finally Sue has to inform Walt about it, as Thao is too shy to speak about it. In order to undo his dishonoring of his own family he has to do odd jobs for Walt as a compensation. It is the first time ever in his life that he succeeds in doing men's work. After the useless first job of counting the birds in a specific tree he begins to shape up the neighborhood. In contrast to Spider's selfishness, Thao works for the community. It is really hard work to repair and paint the neighbors' houses, to get out a tree stump or to remove a wasp nest but Thao meets all challenges. Despite his callous hands he is happy and proud of himself when he goes to Walt's door on his final day. Walt is also pleased with Thao's achievement and realizes he is good at heart.

Thao succeeds in doing men's work

Both get closer when they need each other's help. Thao is unable to repair the faucets and the ceiling fan in his house. Obviously the Lor family cannot afford to have these things fixed. Later Thao can pay back Walt's help by getting up the heavy freezer from his basement. As their friendship intensifies, Walt becomes like a father for Thao. With his height of 1,65 m Bee Vang (acting as Thao) literally looks up to Clint Eastwood who is 1,88 m tall. This is the basis for Walt helping Thao to develop from an insecure youngster into a man. However, according to his mentor, the teenager has to be manned up in his language and behavior. But Thao's first attempt to simply copy the language style of Walt and Martin fails, because at the beginning of his 'education' he is not familiar with the different language registers. Despite of that, he is a quick learner. Taught to follow stereotypical male patterns of talking about women or cars, he is quite successful in his real first test so that he gets a job in construction. Lying to Tim Kennedy (as he has no car whatsoever), he complains about the garage owner:

Helping each other

Thao literally looks up to Walt, his male role model

Talk like a man

> "My head gasket cracked. And the goddamned prick at the shop wants to bend me over for $ 2100." (1:14:42)

Walt teaches him everything he knows and supports him in every respect. Thus he not only provides him with some necessary tools, but also tells him to be more active concerning women. Obviously, Thao takes his advice, because he starts dating Youa. He cannot believe his luck when he is offered the Gran Torino to take her out for dinner.

Thao starts dating Youa

Everything could have been perfect for him if there had not been the gang's claim on him. Considering his upbringing and the general Hmong community's passiveness, it is absolutely convincing that he first accepts the gangbangers' brutality towards him. He explicitly does not want Walt to do anything about it. Only when Spider and Smokie go too far and rape Sue, he comes up with the irrational plan to take revenge and to kill them. Fortunately, Walt calms him down and tricks him into the basement to lock him up. When he is freed by his sister, it is too late. They arrive at the scene only to see that Walt has been killed.

Acceptance of the gang's violence

To Thao's own surprise, Walt passes the vintage car onto him. This is not only the final step in becoming a grown-up man. In a wider context the car opens the door for further assimilation. Given that in the eyes of Americans owning a car is a necessity for success, "Thao is purportedly promised entrance into full-blown American society through Walt's gift of his 1972 Gran Torino" (Jalao 2010, p. 3).

Ending: Thao's big chance for assimilation

Sue
Although Thao's sister Sue is less focused upon in the story, she nevertheless has an important function. Beyond doubt, with her 17 years she is a very self-confident character. The audience does not get to know whether she is going to go "to college" – which would fit in with her general description of Hmong girls – but she is definitely quite smart. Her intellectual superiority to her male counterparts is obvious. This is best shown in her reaction to the African American men who start to harass her. While they get carried away by their lower instincts, focusing on her "tight ass", she alludes to their racial stereotypes and criticizes them for their flawed language:

17-year-old self-confident character

> "Oh, great. Another asshole who has a fetish for Asian girls? God, that gets so old."
> […]
> Of course, right to the stereotype thesaurus. Call me a 'whore' and a 'bitch' in the same sentence." (31:36)

A courageous girl

With respect to the Hmong gangbangers, she does not shy away from any conflict. In contrast to her younger brother Thao, she has the courage to stand up to them. Thus she makes fun of Spider's name and wittily replies to Smokie when she is asked for her age that she is "too old" for him. For apparent reasons, this strategy of playing the intellectual card is quite dangerous. In a way, it is not completely surprising that the gangbangers rape her in order to show their dominant masculine roles over her.

Reasons for Sue's rape

Dating Trey as a sign for her assimilation

As Sue knows what she wants, she does not have any difficulties in living in two worlds. She respects the Hmong traditions, but seems to be quite assimilated into the western world. Quite remarkably, she is dating the white American Trey. Feeling home in both spheres, she is able to bridge the gap between her family and Walt Kowalski. Without her, they would not have become friends. She is the one who invites Walt over and teaches him about Hmong culture. Literally, she is his interpreter for a world unknown to him.

Bridging the gap between two worlds

Phong

Autobiographical experience of the actress

While Sue's and Thao's mother remains a flat character, their grandmother Phong is given some psychological depth. She is a representative of the first-generation immigrants, fleeing communist persecution in 1980. The 61-year-old Chee Thao plays more or less herself. Born in Laos, the actress experienced almost the same fate as her character Phong. Most of her Hmong words were not fixed before, she just said what she found appropriate at the given moment. Bringing in her own story, she is absolutely authentic.

Living according to Hmong traditions

Phong cannot understand why Walt has not left the neighborhood like all the other white people. Similar to him, she has got a lot of racial prejudices. This is no surprise after white America was rather reluctant to support the Hmong by granting them asylum. Phong has not learnt English so that she speaks Hmong throughout the movie. This language barrier has prevented her from integrating into the American lifestyle. Phong lives according to her traditions she brought with her from Asia. This is indicated by her dresses, e.g. her Lao hat, and her spitting out betel nut juice (although some critics observed that Hmong do not chew betel nut; see for example Jalao 2010, p. 1). Like many people in her generation, she still believes in the spiritual power of Kor Khue, the Hmong shaman.

Prejudices against white America

Language barrier

Smokie and Spider

Smokie is the leader of the Hmong gang, but Spider sticks out as a prominent member as well. All the others lack any individuality. Their usual way of rebellion is terrorizing the neighborhood. The gangbangers follow their own rules, meeting no resistance from the Hmong community. Most of them are so much intimidated that nobody dares to talk to the police. Even when Sue is raped, nobody is willing to give a hint. Father Janovich works with some of the Hmong gangs, but his efforts seem to be pointless.

Rebellion against their father's culture

No resistance against terrorizing the neighborhood

In contrast to Thao's hard working ethics, Smokie and his gang are unemployed. They do not want to be Americanized or aim at being given access to society, but rather follow their own rules. For them, it is important to defend their territory, e.g. against rivaling gangs. Within their own community, they are eager to save face. Any disobedience will be punished. That's why they cannot leave Thao alone and press a lit cigarette into his cheek to publicly show their dominance.

Unemployment of the gangbangers

Another logic they follow is returning any hostile action against them. They are used to a spiral of violence, every time claiming a higher prize in reaction to what was done to them. Thus it is clear that Walt's beating up of Smokie must be answered by an act causing more pain and warning the other ones not to go on any further. For this reason, they do not try to kill anybody in their drive-by shooting. It is meant to be a last warning. Sue, however, is punished brutally by them.

Following their own rules of violence and retaliation

"The boys go to jail"

In the end "the boys go to jail", as described by Sue earlier. They are trapped by Walt who has come unarmed in order to leave no questions about their guilt. Thus the shootout resembles an execution. Under these circumstances, and as there are several witnesses, the gangbangers will probably be imprisoned for the rest of their lives.

Father Janovich

> **INFO AT A GLANCE**
>
> **An inexperienced "over-educated, 27-year-old virgin" learns about life and death**
> - The Catholic Irishman delivers an impersonal eulogy for Dorothy Kowalski.
> - He tries very hard to remove the veteran's wall of bitterness and shame, but for a long time he does not get through to him.
> - Walt's direct way of telling him his opinion and his hidden war experiences change Father Janovich's outlook on life.
> - It is quite a step for him to show some understanding for Thao's wish to kill the gangbangers.
> - After Walt's confession, Father Janovich calls the police to prevent the almost inevitable shootout.
> - In the sermon at Walt's funeral he publicly acknowledges Walt Kowalski's influence on him.

Detached from his congregation

Striking age difference

Inconvincing rhetoric of the seminary

Father Janovich is introduced in the opening scene of Dorothy Kowalski's funeral. He is quite detached from the congregation of mourners which is mainly due to the church's architecture and the funeral arrangements, but his distance has a symbolic quality as well. As he seems to be very young, he is probably not the suitable person to comfort the old Walt and his family. Saying that death is "bittersweet" and his academic questions "What is death?" and "What is life?" do not show any empathy. They belong to the standard rhetoric of the seminary, but rather reveal Father Janovich's inexperience with the main topics of life.

Dorothy's wish: Walt should go to confession

However, he takes his profession seriously. He definitely wants to fulfill Dorothy Kowalski's last wish that her husband goes to confession. Unfortunately, he has no idea how to communicate with the widower. His attempts to establish some personal relationship by calling him "Walt" utterly fail. Christopher Carley, who plays Father

Janovich, once stated in jest that his sole function seems to ring at Walt's door only to see Clint Eastwood smashing it in his face (cf. chapter 3). Walt is not at all impressed by the priest's pastoral task. He confronts him in his own, direct way with his view that Father Janovich is an "over-educated, 27-year-old virgin", only good for superstitious old ladies and that he would never confess to a "boy that's just out of the seminary."

Harsh criticism

Nevertheless, Walt is impressed by the priest's persistence. Father Janovich even looks for him at the bar, quite an unusual location for a serious talk with one "sheep of his flock". The priest wants to stick to his abstinence, but Walt does not accept this, and so he orders a gin and tonic instead of a diet coke. Then they exchange their views on "life and death", obviously the Father's favorite subject. Walt tells him about the horrific war experiences he has to live with. This somehow breaks the ice between the two.

Talk about "life and death" at the bar

Father Janovich also works with some of the Hmong gangs, so when he gets to know that Walt saved Thao he pays a visit to the old man. His question why the veteran did not call the police is ridiculed by Walt who pretends to have prayed for their coming. However, the priest's following passionate speech that stronger men than Walt have found relief in confessing their sins has a somewhat astonishing effect. Voluntarily the veteran tells the priest that some men (possibly meaning he himself) are most haunted by those things they were not ordered to do.

"I'm impressed, you came with your guns loaded"

Walt's painful lessons about "life and death" change the "padre", as he is called by the old veteran. When the Korean ex-soldier asks him what he would do in Thao's place after his sister's rape, Father Janovich admits that he would take revenge. He fully understands that the Hmong teenager expects Walt to be at his side. Personally he would of course refrain from any violence, but it is a big step for him not to reject any retaliation rigorously. His change is underlined by him having a beer. In contrast to his former preference for non-alcoholic drinks he takes two cans for each of them from the ice chest.

Father Janovich changes

71

Analysis and Interpretation

Fear of the worst

All the same, he is very surprised when Walt comes to church to ask him for a confession the following day. In particular when the veteran tells him that he is at peace now, Father Janovich knows that some disaster is going to happen. Therefore he calls the police and waits in front of the gangbangers' house. However, the policemen force him to leave after hours of waiting without Walt turning up. When the priest returns there at nightfall, it is too late. His later eulogy for Walt Kowalski shows that he has learnt a lot. He publicly acknowledges the veteran's importance for his personal development.

Themes

Racism in a Multicultural Society

INFO AT A GLANCE

"Hope for a Racist, and Maybe a Country" (Dargis)
- *Gran Torino* questions the ideal of white America.
- The movie shows a racially segregated society.
- Despite its frequent racial slurs, *Gran Torino* has a strong anti-racist message.
- Nevertheless, the movie has also been criticized for confirming racial stereotypes.

The cultural mix shown in the movie does not reflect reality

Gran Torino gives an interesting insight into U.S. multicultural society. Although the displayed cultural mix does not reflect reality (more than 90% of Highland Park's inhabitants are African Americans), the movie shows the contribution of different ethnic groups to American society and gives a clue to some general population trends. Apart from the groups relevant for the plot, the scene with Walt's visit to the doctor is most interesting. She is of Asian descent and has replaced the

At the doctor's

white American doctor Walt used to see. Quite remarkably, she has a Muslim assistant, a rather small but fast growing minority in the U.S. In the waiting-room Walt is the only white person. The other patients seem to be from various cultural backgrounds, showing the diversity of the population.

The movie questions the ideal of a conservative white America, which obviously is not able to represent the country anymore. At the beginning of the Obama era, the U.S.A. has developed into a more colorful country than Walt's generation had ever expected, not to say feared. Walt Kowalski considers himself a true American. Part of his national identity is driving American cars and having a flag on his porch. However, *Gran Torino* shows that this kind of nationalism is a flawed concept. Walt is no more or no less a true American than everybody else, as he is a Polish immigrant. The barber is an Italian, Father Janovich and the construction supervisor Tim Kennedy are of Irish descent.

Questioning the conservative ideal of white America

As far as interracial discourse and relationships are concerned, the movie shows a rather gloomy picture. The presented society at the beginning of the movie is racially clearly segregated. Whites, Asians and Blacks live their lives in parallel societies in their own neighborhoods. With the decline of the automobile industry, whites have left Highland Park. Only Walt Kowalski, his wife and the woman living opposite him have resisted the well-known phenomenon of white flight. Instead, Hmong people moved in, forming an Asian exclave in which they follow their own traditions and speak their own language. African Americans, represented by the three young men harassing Sue obviously have their own different "territory".

Gloomy picture of a segregated society

White flight

It is clearly shown that people stick to their own kind. An exception to this implicit social norm is Sue who is dating Trey. Walt has internalized this rule, so that on his ride in his truck together with Sue he asks her:

Social norm: Stick to your own kind

> "And what about that goofball guy you were with? Is that a date or something? [...] Well, you shouldn't be hanging out with him. You should be hanging out with your own people, with other ... Humongs!" (35:02)

Thus, though living in the same city, the different races or ethnic groups do not have much in common, but rather meet with distrust and prejudices. If they actually bump into each other, dangerous conflicts arise. This can be seen in Sue's harassment as well as in the scene where

Traditional concepts do not mirror reality	the Hmong and Latino gangs almost pull their triggers. The salad bowl, a concept for describing American society, does not seem to be an adequate image for the presented social reality any more. The 13-letter traditional motto appearing e.g. on the Great Seal of the United States "E pluribus unum" (Latin for "Out of many, one") seems to be a somewhat outdated ideal.
Neighbors do not have any contact to each other	Even if people of different cultures live next door to each other, there is no contact or exchange. There is no one of the Hmong neighbors present at Dorothy Kowalski's funeral or at the following feast at home. Thao only comes to ask for jumper cables, although he must have noticed that someone died next door. Walt is no better. He just asks himself, "[h]ow many swamp rats can you get in one room?", not realizing that people are invited for a special occasion. Language barriers play a major role, because they block communication between the different ethnic groups. This is most obvious in the antagonism of Walt and Phong who do not speak each other's language.
Language barriers	
Misconceptions and ignorance	Misconceptions, based on ignorance, can be found on all sides. Trey, Sue's boyfriend, seems to believe that African Americans permanently address each other as "bro". Furthermore, he is obviously of the opinion that he as a white man can copy that in order to fraternize with the African American peers. Thao thinks he can call Martin names in the same way as Walt, although the Italian barber is a complete stranger to him. Not surprisingly, prejudices against the other groups are widespread. *Gran Torino* shows how these are reiterated in one's in-group, e.g. by Walt's joke told to his war buddies:

> "There's a Mexican, a Jew and a colored guy go into a bar. The bartender looks up and says: 'Get the fuck out of here.'"
> (17:26)

Origin of Walt's racism	The movie also reveals in which contexts racial prejudices originate. In Walt's case it is in the Korean War, in which he fought Koreans and Chinese, probably unable to distinguish between the two. Generalizing his experience, he has called all Asians "gooks" or "zipperheads" – as all soldiers did at that time – until the

present day. Phong's hatred of white America probably results from the reluctance of the United States to care for the Hmong people after the Vietnam War.

Walt's racism is clearly directed against the Hmong neighbors. Despite his massive violation of political correctness, American audiences commented his racial slurs with big laughs. This is probably due to the fact that Asian Americans have a rather positive image. Interestingly, he does not call the African Americans "nigger" or anything worse, as this would have probably caused a different reaction in the audience. By showing that Walt can overcome his racial prejudices, the movie "carries a strong anti-racist message" (http://chadwickfilm. wordpress.com/2010/01/31/what-messages-does-gran-torino-convey, 8 April 2017).

Gran Torino reveals that racism creates a divide between different ethnic groups and causes violence. At the core of Walt's racism, there is his egocentric inability to analyze himself. He has always complained about others, believing in their faults instead of asking what he himself can do to change the situation. The contact with his Hmong neighbors enables him to get a certain amount of introspection and gives him a second chance. Although he continues with his racist language until the end, his behavior shows that he has changed his attitude. Choosing between two life paths (cf. his horoscope), he seems to take the right direction. However, if an emotionally-hardened racist like Walt Kowalski can achieve this, then there is hope maybe for the whole country (cf. Dargis 2008). The message is to accept the ongoing changes in society and to acknowledge the diversity of the country.

> "'Gran Torino' is about two things, I believe. It's about the belated flowering of a man's better nature. And it's about Americans of different races growing more open to one another in the new century. This doesn't involve some kind of grand transformation. It involves starting to see the "gooks" next door as people you love. And it helps if you live in the kind of neighbourhood where they are next door." (Ebert 2008, "Gran Torino: Get off my lawn"; https://2engom.wikispaces. com/file/view/%27Gran+Torin0%27+Task+Booklet.pdf)

Margin notes:
- Reactions of the audience to violation of political correctness
- "Strong anti-racist message"
- Need for introspection
- "Hope for a Racist, and May be a Country"

Analysis and Interpretation

Confirmation of negative stereotypes	Despite the movie's general appraisal, it has also been criticized for confirming lots of stereotypes. This is particularly true for the African Americans who are presented as hanging around in the street and attacking every girl they meet. There is a widespread fear of white America towards black males, which is reinforced by the national media on a daily basis. Maybe surprisingly, there were also complaints about the representation of the Hmong. In accordance with their general image in the media, Asian Americans are portrayed in *Gran Torino* as docile and passive, even effeminate. They are helpless against the gang's terrorizing the neighborhood. According to these (mainly Asian) voices, it is typical of Hollywood movies that Asian Americans need a white person to solve their problems. The same applies to
Assimilation	certain positive stereotypes such as the widespread assumption that Asian girls are smart or that Asians take great effort in assimilating. Whereas Sue seems to be well-integrated into American society from the beginning, Thao needs Walt's help. With the 1972 Gran Torino he
Positive ending	has finally got some essential requirement for his future success. His traveling alongside Lake St. Clair therefore definitely is a positive ending.

(Gun) Violence

> **INFO AT A GLANCE**
>
> **The right to bear arms**
> - The Second Amendment to the Constitution grants every citizen the right to bear arms.
> - It is a hotly disputed issue in the United States.
> - Walt Kowalski has at least two guns: his M1 Grand Rifle from the Korean War and a pistol. He does not hesitate to take them in order to scare the gang-bangers away.
> - The Latino and Hmong gangs use their guns for enforcing dominance or committing crimes.
> - *Gran Torino* is an example of the dynamics of violence and the acceleration of reprisals.

The founding fathers of the United States granted the citizens the right to bear arms. This right was given in a time when the authorities were far away and a weapon at hand was the only way to survive in the wilderness. Beyond doubt, having a gun became a tradition deeply rooted in the American self-image. Today is it believed that there is a gun in every second household in the U.S.

An American tradition

However, two and half centuries after the Second Amendment to the Constitution this has become a hotly disputed issue. In particular after a series of mass shootings, the Democrats are in favor of restricting that right. However, the powerful National Rifle Association (NRA) and the Republicans block any reform. This is why, until the present day, it is very easy to get access to guns and ammunition.

NRA and Republicans vs Democrats

The consequences of this American tradition are quite obvious in *Gran Torino*. Walt Kowalski owns at least two guns. He brought his M1 Garand Rifle home from the Korean War five decades ago. Due to his care (cf. his preparation for the final shootout) it is in mint condition after all those years. On the other hand, he has bought a pistol which is shown in the scene with the African Americans. Whereas the rifle is stored in some special box in his house, he seems to carry the pistol with him when he goes out. This is the only explanation why he has it at hand when he needs it to save Sue. However,

M1 Garand Rifle from Korea

Walt uses his guns more or less as deterrents to prevent others from attacking

the rifle is also ready to be loaded, e.g. to protect himself against a burglar. This is shown in the scene when he gets it out in the middle of the night after he heard some noise in his garage. There is no question that Walt would use one of these weapons in self-defense. This is also definitely his primary motivation when he interferes in the gang's conflict with Thao's family. Quite remarkably, except for his unintentional shot in the garage which is rather a result of his tripping and falling on the ground than an attempt to shoot down Thao, he never actually pulls the trigger. He uses the guns as a threat only, as a means to scare away his enemies or to keep them at a distance.

The drive-by shooting: final warning and demonstration of power

The gangs, on the other hand, use their guns in a different way. In their direct confrontation the Latino gangbanger flashes a pistol without any necessity, just to show his power. As a response, Smokie pulls out a sub-machine gun to reassure the dominance of the Hmong gang. It is unclear whether both gangs are ready to use their weapons, as the Latinos give in and drive away. That the Hmong gangbangers do not refrain from using their guns, becomes obvious in their drive-by shooting. In this scene they use their weapons as a final warning. Until this moment they do not aim at killing anybody. However, provoked by Walt, they shoot him down mercilessly.

Various levels of violence in Gran Torino

Latent violence (verbal tensions)

Overall, *Gran Torino* shows various levels of violence. At the beginning there are only verbal tensions between the different groups and Walt. Aggressive exchanges can also be seen with his family, Thao and Father Janovich. The language barrier between Walt and Phong does not prevent them from acting out their mutual disdain. Until that moment, latent violence can only be perceived between pairs of individuals. The next stage is the level of gang violence which introduces the appearance of guns for the first time. Walt Kowalski continues to embody the principle of violence as he turns up with a gun in his hand to save Thao. A little later, he feigns pulling the trigger with his fingers, before actually producing a gun in front of the African American men. All of these actions take place in the absence of any mediating person who could prevent the rising level of violence. Indeed, until almost to the end of the movie, the police are not seen on the spot.

In a way, Walt keeps on breeding violence by separating Thao from the Hmong gang. Instead of minding his own business, he teaches Thao to become an American man and causes anger and hatred. *Gran Torino* perfectly displays the mechanisms and dynamics of the unfolding spiral of violence.

Mechanisms and dynamics of the spiral of violence

> "Everything starts with the response – a response that was bound to come – from the Hmong band. The response begins by being centered on Thao, who suffers a new kind of – 'initiation' at the hands of the gang. […], but one now closer to the pure form of violence, in which a pack of men encircle und punish a single man. At that moment the vicious cycle of violence finally accelerates: *until then, physical violence had never existed*. There had been only verbal violence and simulations of weapons being fired. […] The cycle will unfold in an accelerating crescendo." (Machuco 2011; http://anthropoetics.ucla.edu/ap1602/1602machuco/)

Responses and acceleration

Walt replies to Thao's burn by raising the stakes. He waits for Smokie until he is alone and beats him brutally. It seems to be typical of the logic of reprisals that the action moves from the center to the periphery. The Hmong gangbangers do not attack Walt, who is their central opponent, but unleash their revenge at the more vulnerable periphery, Thao's family. In their drive-by shooting the escalation of violence continues. At this point, the movie speeds up dramatically. Sue returns brutally beaten and raped. The Korean War veteran begins to understand his share in the vicious cycle. He understands that Thao expects him to raise the stakes again and kill the gang. Even the audience expects a final shootout. "What else could be 'expected' from someone with Clint Eastwood's record" (Machuco 2011), after his memorable roles such as "Dirty Harry"? Not 24 hours after the gang's brutal acts Walt publicly confronts Smokie and his followers in front of their house. Walt's self-sacrifice surprises the viewer but is consistent with the character and the overall plot. It is Walt's own way to stop the cycle of violence. He dies so that others can live.

Attack on the periphery: Thao's family

End of violence in a surprise ending

Expectations

Analysis and Interpretation

Concepts of Masculinity

INFO AT A GLANCE

Guns, cars, girls and a tough language
- Walt Kowalski's characterization corresponds to the traditional definitions of masculinity.
- He went to war and possesses two guns.
- He worked at Ford and has two cars: a pickup truck and the Gran Torino.
- He married and raised a family with two sons.
- Walt drinks a lot and is a chain-smoker.
- His language is vulgar and commanding.
- In contrast to Walt, Thao Vang Lor is bossed around by his sister and does women's work.
- Other Hmong teenagers are gangbangers, rebelling against their culture and their fathers' way of life.
- With Walt's help, Thao is manned up: He is taught to talk like a man and starts dating Youa.
- He gets a job in construction, a field considered to be typically male.
- When the Gran Torino is passed over to him, his assimilation to American society is completed.

Male identity shaped by social expectations

Concepts of masculinity are unwritten, but widely accepted notions of how men should be like. Shaped by expectations of both men and women, these concepts influence men's behavior and become part of their identity. Obviously, they change in the course of time. Nowadays in western culture, men are expected to be softer, to be more understanding and to be more present in their families than before.

Soldier in Korea

However, as far as traditional definitions of masculinity are concerned, Walt Kowalski seems to be a perfect example. In short, in *Gran Torino* these concepts focus on guns, cars, girls and a tough language. As a young man, Walt went to Korea to fight against communism. At that time, being a soldier was a man's "privilege". Discipline, being hard to oneself and showing no weakness were the central necessities taught to young soldiers which definitely shaped their later lives. Walt learnt to suppress his feelings and to conceal his bad conscience for decades. The war taught him to act quickly in order to survive, not to rely on others and to solve his problems alone.

The importance of serving his country can also be seen in Walt's bringing home his M1 Grand Rifle. The movie proves that he did not only take it as souvenir, but as the most effective means of protecting himself. It is a symbol of his – rather typically male – idea that that you must not rely on others for help. Additionally, he has bought a pistol at some later stage which he can always take with him.

M1 Garand Rifle

Self-reliance and self-defense

An essential part of Walt's male identity is his working at a Ford factory for almost his entire life. It was his job to put the steering column in the Gran Torino. He seems not to drive his own vintage car anymore which motor experts – due to the Gran Torino's enormous horsepower – usually call a "muscle car". For his daily rides he has got a pickup truck which is considered to be a male car as well, since it allows to transport goods from one place to the other without having to call a professional company.

Working at Ford

Two "masculine" cars

Walt's machines and tools underline his masculinity as well and show that he is a handyman. His old-fashioned lawn-mower is hand-operated and needs manpower. His collection of tools in his garage not only impresses Thao, but would make most men envious. With these tools, Walt is able to do all chores by himself, whether it is fixing the faucets or dealing with the ceiling fan.

Hand-operated lawn-mower and impressive tool collection

Following the general expectations of the 1950s, Walt married and raised a family. With his two sons he probably had a model American family. While he worked at Ford, his wife stayed at home. This might be one reason for his difficulties to develop a close relationship with them which he now obviously regrets. His credo has always been to treat women with respect. This can be seen by the way he gets along with Sue. As most men of his age Walt seems to be convinced that men have to be more active than women, especially when it comes to getting into touch. In this context he explains to Thao:

Model American family

Male/female gender roles

> "I may not be the most pleasant person to be around, but I got the best woman that was ever on this planet to marry me. I worked at it. It was the best thing that ever happened to me." (50:46)

Analysis and Interpretation

Excessive smoking and drinking

Whether it was his wife's wish that Walt never had a cigarette in the house, remains unclear. Anyhow, with "snow on the ground near half the year", it must have been quite hard for the chain-smoker to have his cigarettes outside throughout the year. His excessive smoking and drinking habits are by no means only gap-filling, but again stress his stereotypically male attitude.

Last but not least, there is Walt's language which must be considered as typically male. Women would not use the same vulgar diction which the following example shows:

> Walt
> Come on, get the shit out of your mouth. Tell me what you want?
>
> Thao
> Do you have any jumper cables? My uncle's car is old and …
>
> Walt
> No, we don't have any jumper cables. And have some respect, zipperhead. We're in mourning here. (7:13)

Commanding tone

Obviously, Walt's mode of expression goes along with overt racism in this case. However, he talks to other whites in the same way which can be seen in a conversation with Father Janovich at the Veteran's bar. When the priest wants to order a Diet Coke, Walt commands: "Bullshit. This is a bar. You have a drink." This tone is quite typical of him (cf. "Get off my lawn") and must be interpreted as another sign of his masculinity.

Martin, the Italian barber

Walt's visits to the Italian barber show that he is used to strange, but common exchanges between men in which they call each other names. Obviously, it is some kind of game between the two of them (cf. the frequent reference to their countries of origin: "dump Italian-Wop-Dago" vs. "old Pollack son of a bitch"). In general, the barber serves as another example of an adult man. When he has no customers, he reads men's magazines thus supporting the idea that male identity has to do with being interested in nude photographs. Like Walt, Martin has got a rifle, which he produces out of the blue when Thao tries to copy their language style.

The Hmong teenager, on the other hand, is still seeking for his identity. With his sandals and socks he does not look very masculine. Neither has he a grown a beard. He is criticized for being bossed around and doing work which is considered to be women's duty, e.g. washing the dishes. Interestingly, the accusation to act more like a woman than a man is pronounced by persons from different generations and cultures. Thao's grandmother Phong is the first to speak it out publicly. Walt keeps on calling him "pussy", because he is passive and docile.

Thao's search for his male identity

Thao's indecisiveness as to which gender concepts he should abide by is even more striking if one looks at his male peer group. Those who are shown in *Gran Torino* have banded together in various gangs, depending on which they belong to. They hang around in the street (African Americans) or drive around in their cars, listening to their favorite music (Latinos, Hmong). None of them seems to have a job, and most often they tend to sexual harassment. With their vulgar mode of expression their language resembles that of Walt and other male adults. In case of the Hmong whose behavior is described in more detail, the group members teach each other in their masculine identity by setting up initiation rituals or following their leaders. They live up to their own rules, not accepting any authorities anymore. It is a rebellion against their fathers who have lost their function as role models.

Contrast to his male peers

Rebellious Hmong gang-bangers

At the beginning, Thao misses everything which he considers necessary for his successful male identity. According to his own analysis, he does not "have a job or a car or a girlfriend." Walt helps him with all of these problems. However, before he can tackle any of these, Thao has to be manned up in his language first. Who could that do better than Martin and he himself? They teach him "to bitch about [his] girlfriend or getting [his] car fixed", two stereotypically male topics.

Thao does not have a "job or a car or a girlfriend"

Obviously, the movie hangs on to male and female clichés, as the following example illustrates in which Martin complains about the failing communication between him and his wife:

Analysis and Interpretation

Male and female stereotypes	"Or, my old lady bitches for two goddamn hours about how they don't take expired coupons at the grocery store and the minute I turn on the fucking game, she starts crying how we never talk." (1:12:07)
	Shortly afterwards Walt takes Thao to the construction superintendant ("the super"). When asked why he has no car, Thao shows that he has learnt his lesson. He lies to Tim Kennedy and tells him that he has been cheated at a repair shop, a comment which the super takes up immediately and complains about his own experiences of being ripped off for getting his car repaired. The job interview seems to prove the underlying conception that men's topics focus on girls and cars only.
Girlfriend and the Gran Torino	Alongside with his job, the teenager is successful in finding a girlfriend. It is quite significant that Youa also takes part in the American barbecue in Walt's backyard. Apparently, Thao has followed the veteran's advice in inviting Youa for dinner and a movie afterwards. With Walt's generous offer to take the Gran Torino, Thao – at least temporarily – possesses everything he needs for his successful career as an American. When Walt finally passes the car onto him in his last will, Thao's development from a teenager to a male adult is completed.

Generation Gaps

INFO AT A GLANCE

Materialistic interests vs. social values
- Walt and Mitch Kowalski do not only differ in their physical appearance, but also in their mentalities. Mitch is a typical representative of the post-war generation whose capitalist ideas are questioned and criticized.
- The sons do not have time for their father.
- The relationship between Walt and his grandchildren seems to be even worse. In particular his granddaughter Ashley shows no respect for him.
- In contrast to Walt's grandchildren, Thao and Sue look up to him. They are similar to him in that they appreciate traditions and social ties.
- For Thao, Walt becomes a mentor or teacher and a bit of a father.
- Young Father Janovich also learns a lot about life and death from the Korean War veteran.

There are several generation gaps to be seen in *Gran Torino*. One the one hand the movie focuses on Walt and his sons Mitch and Steve. Probably even more important is the relation between the 78-year-old protagonist and the generation of American and Hmong teenagers. Last but not least there is a contrast between the Korean War veteran and the young inexperienced Father Janovich.

Obviously, Walt has a closer relationship with his eldest son Mitch than with second-born Steve who is only present at the two funerals. Throughout the movie he does not phone his father nor does Walt try to get into touch with him. Both his sons are completely different from their father. Even in their physical appearance they do not seem to have anything in common. Whereas Walt is slim, Dargis (2008) describes his two sons and their lifestyle with the words "big houses, big cars, big waistlines." In contrast to Walt who has always been a worker in the automobile industry, his sons seem to be superficial yuppies living in the richer residential districts. Walt's house is rather small, offering no luxury, whereas the kitchen-isle in the middle of Mitch's spacious home suggests a comfortable way of living. Moreover,

Mitch and Steve

"Big houses, big cars, big waistlines"

> "his two grown sons are anti-Eastwood figures of masculinity: weak, ineffectual men, dominate by their shrewish, materialistic wives." (http://www.rascismreview.com/blog/2009/01/17/gran-torino-white-masculinity-racism)

"Weak men"

Analysis and Interpretation

Working at Ford and owning a Gran Torino vs. driving a Toyota

Additionally, there is a big gap in the mentality of the different generations. Walt's patriotism is not only shown by his having an American flag on his porch, but also by preferring American products. As a former Ford employee, it is natural for him to have a car of that company. He cannot understand that his own son sells Toyotas and drives a Toyota Land Cruiser. One could imagine that Walt's predominant association with regard to Japanese cars is the attack on Pearl Harbor 60 years before. Mitch, on the other hand, has grown up in a globalized world in which everybody looks after himself, making profits with national and international products likewise.

Focused on money

In general, Mitch, his brother and their families seem to be mainly oriented towards money and their own (financial) advantage. Mitch phones his father only if he wants something from him. Despite the son's alleged interest in his father's well-being, Walt is suspicious of Mitch's real purpose of calling him. As he remarks, it cannot be Dorothy's jewelry as his wife Karen went through all of it before. Indeed it turns out that the sole reason for calling is to ask for season tickets for the local football team. As a reaction, Walt hangs up. When he himself phones his son sometime later, presumably wishing to tell Mitch about his fatal disease, Mitch is busy with bills. Just before Walt might have taken the courage to reveal his problem, Mitch suggests calling him again on the weekend. Materialistic interests prevent an overdue conversation between father and son.

Mitch is busy with bills

Sons have no time for their father

Obviously, Walt has had to learn that his sons do not have time for him. This painful experience is expressed in various scenes in *Gran Torino*, starting off with Walt's harsh remark that he rather gets the chairs from the basement himself before it is done by his son "next week". Although it would have been natural to stay at the funeral feast until the very end, Mitch leaves as early as possible, giving the excuse that the "kids are getting restless." No wonder that Walt turned into a bitter old man, alienated from his sons.

Certainly he is not an easy person to live with, but Clint Eastwood makes the audience sympathize with Walt Kowalski. The viewer puts the blame for the difficult family relations rather on the sons and their wives. Above all, the viewer's bias against Walt's family members is confirmed in the scene on Walt's birthday when Mitch and his wife Karen have brought gifts which are absolutely out of place. Despite his sound physical condition they treat him as more in need of care than is actually the case.

Audience sympathizes with Walt

On the whole, Mitch's and Steve's portrayal tends to be quite negative. Their typically American way of life is questioned and criticized throughout the movie. Their greed for money is finally expressed in the scene when Walt's last will is opened. One can see from the facial expressions of all the family members present that they expect the veteran to have passed the house and his other belongings to their sons.

Negative portrayal of the American way of life

As the apple never falls far from the tree, Ashley and Josh follow their parents' patterns. The story focuses on Walt's granddaughter who is portrayed as a rather unlikable person right from the start. Although she must have known that her grandfather would have liked to see her in decent clothes in order to show respect for the ceremony, she appears with a bare and pierced belly button. Probably everybody understands Walt's growling at her sight in the church. Obviously she has not had any deeper relationship with her dead grandmother since she does not show any signs of emotional involvement. Ashley is just bored as there is no connectivity to the Internet in her grandfather's house. In contrast to Thao and Sue, she and her brother seem to be addicted to their smartphones and the social media. Even during the church service she is distracted by these things. Later, when Walt phones Mitch, both of the teenagers are shown playing around with their smartphones as well.

Unsympathetic Ashley

Addicted to her smartphone

In many other respects, Ashley is a typical representative of her generation. Like the three teenager who only make fun of Walt's neighbor when she spills her

Critical portrait of Ashley's generation

groceries, Ashley does not help her grandfather, e.g. getting up some chairs from the basement. Whether Walt does not understand this lack of respect towards grown-ups or has just accepted it or grown used to it, remains unclear.

Secretly Ashley takes a smoke in Walt's garage. Similar to many teenagers, she probably does not want her parents to know that she started smoking. Seeing the Gran Torino makes her dream of having such a cool "vintage" car. Quite shockingly, she probably wishes her grandfather dead as soon as possible:

Ashley's lack of empathy

> "So … what are you gonna do with it, when you, like, die?" (6:37)

In her materialist worldview, she is only interested in what she can get from Walt. Cold-hearted, she plans ahead, so that she makes no secret out of her interest in the "super cool retro couch" for her room when she goes to college the following year.

No real communication

Ashley neither understands Walt's emotional connection to the Gran Torino, nor his traditional values. Walt comments her questions with irony and contempt ("You've probably just painted your nails"), but they never engage in a proper conversation. It is beyond doubt that Ashley expects to inherit the Gran Torino. This is the logical consequence of her past claims. However, Walt follows his own social logic in that he gives everything to the church and his "friend" Thao.

Hmong sense of community

Everything Walt misses in his own family, he finds with his Hmong neighbors. Like him, they live according to their cultural traditions. The Hmong community seems to be a lively social network, taking part in each other's destinies. Although it is difficult to decide who belongs to the Lor family and who is just a member of the Hmong neighborhood, all show a remarkable sense of community. In contrast to the rather scattered people at Walt's funeral feast, the Hmong collectively celebrate the birth ceremony. After Walt has saved Thao, one of their members, all of them express their gratefulness to the white old man by bringing gifts to his porch. In a later scene a lot of them are invited to the Lor family's house for a barbecue. It has to be assumed that similar gatherings take place at other Hmong houses as well.

As a lonesome widower Walt does not only appreciate their general social ties, but is particularly surprised by the intergenerational relations. The youngsters treat the elder Hmong with respect. They accept the experiences and wisdom of the old. Regardless of their age, all Hmong believe in the authority of the shaman, the spiritual leader of their community. He speaks out what has been unsaid for decades in Walt's own family.

<small>Respect for the old</small>

Being more or less the same age, Thao and Sue are directly juxtaposed to Walt's grandchildren. Whereas Ashley is a "self-centred greed machine" (Ebert 2008), Thao does odd jobs for the community. In contrast to Ashley's addiction to the social media, he enjoys reading books which can be seen when he bumps into the Latino gang. In opposition to Thao who looks up to Walt, Ashley looks down on him. She dresses disrespectfully at Dorothy's funeral, while Thao appears in his traditional costume at Walt's funeral.

<small>Thao and Sue are juxtaposed to Ashley and Josh</small>

In the Hmong's adherence to their cultural roots, their sense of community and their respectful treatment of the old, the Korean War veteran recognizes common social values. It is quite natural that his neighbors become a family substitute for the old man. Like a father, he takes the 16-year-old teenager Thao under his wing. His connection to the Hmong is best seen when he invites Thao, Sue and their mother to an American barbecue in his backyard. Emotionally, he establishes unusual links to his Asian neighbors. He calls Thao a "friend", but considering that he sacrifices himself and passes his most precious thing – the Gran Torino – onto him, this connection must be rather interpreted as a father-and-son relationship in the end.

<small>Substitute father takes Thao under his wing</small>

Finally, there is a clear generational gap between Walt Kowalski and Father Janovich. The veteran has had to learn bitter lessons about life and death, starting in the Korean War and ending with his wife's recent death.

<small>Walt and Father Janovich</small>

Thus he cannot accept the standardized phrases of the seminary which the priest uses. Father Janovich is definitely too young for being a good consultant. He lacks credibility, as he is inexperienced in life. However, the Father's persistence impresses Walt and they have great influence on one another. Despite his reserve against the Catholic Church, the veteran opens his heart and finally confesses to the priest. Apparently, most important is what he does not reveal to him, but the Catholic minister is able to come to the correct conclusions and tries to prevent bloodshed. The church inherits Walt's house, definitely a result of his acknowledgment of Father Janovich's engagement. The priest, on the other side, learns a lot about the painful losses everybody has to meet in life. Both benefit from their relationship.

Guilt and Redemption

INFO AT A GLANCE

Walt's twofold guilt
- In the Korean War Walt killed about 13 people.
- He is particularly haunted by his murdering an innocent Korean teenager.
- More than 50 years later he is responsible for the escalation of violence in his neighborhood, including Sue's rape.
- He tries to atone for his twofold guilt by sacrificing himself.
- His redemption is expressed by the symbol of the cross when he is shot down.

Atrocities in the Korean War

The Korean War (1950–1953) was led with outspoken cruelty. Atrocities and war crimes could be found on either side. One of the worst massacres committed by the American troops was the killing of several hundred civilians at No Gun Ri (1950). Officers are reported to have explicitly ordered to kill all fleeing people including women and children. In his conversations with Father Janovich Walt reveals his own limited point of view of the general warfare:

Walt's war experiences

"I lived for almost three years in Korea with it [death]. We shot men, stabbed them with bayonets, hacked seventeen-year-olds to death with shovels. Stuff I'll remember till the day I die. Horrible things, but things I'll live with." (19:10)

The Koreans were dehumanized, labeled as "swamp rats" and used as "sandbags" which could be "stacked [...] five feet high." Individual soldiers even went beyond their orders, torturing and killing randomly "chinks" of every age. Walt admits that he personally killed 13 people, "maybe more." But what haunts him most, is what he was not ordered to do. In particular, he cannot forget his shooting an innocent Korean teenager who just wanted to give up. More than fifty years he has lived with that guilt. His bad conscience has reminded him of his crimes every single day thereafter. Presumably, he never told that to anybody before. Due to his inner distance to the Catholic Church he did not go to confession, either, but preferred not to show his true feelings.

Dehumanizaton of the so-called enemies

Walt's personal guilt

As the plot develops, Walt Kowalski realizes that he is also guilty for the brutalities done to Sue. He is the one who has taken revenge on Smokie after his burning a cigarette into Thao's cheek. There cannot be any doubt that he is responsible for the spiral of violence because he must have known that the Hmong gang would react. Walt punishes himself by hurting his hands, the "weapons" he used to beat up the gang's leader. But he knows that this is not enough to pay off his guilt. This time he cannot go on without any compensation, this time calls for a real sacrifice.

Responsible for the retaliation spiral

Punishing himself is not enough

It is quite plausible to assume that he draws a direct line from his Korean War crimes to his moral responsibility in 2008. He is not used to distinguish between Koreans, Chinese or Hmong, for him they are all alike. His neighbors must have reminded him of his deeds every day. In his point of view, his twofold guilt towards Asians cannot be retaliated by a shootout in which he executes the gangbangers. His lifelong guilt can only be atoned for by sacrificing himself. Probably it is not really important that Walt is about to die anyway due to his lung cancer. One has to assume that he would have acted the same without his fatal disease. For him, the opportunity to atone for his crimes and failures offers one of the "second chances", which were announced in his horoscope. With his self-sacrifice, he finally is at peace with himself.

Sacrificing his life in order to atone for his twofold guilt

"Second chances"

Analysis and Interpretation

Allusions to Christ's death	Walt knows exactly what he is doing. As he once got "blood on his hands", he plans to deal with the gangbangers alone. He does not want to spoil Thao's life who has a promising future ahead of him. Deliberately Walt goes unarmed to the gangbangers' house. His Christ-like figure in the moment of death reminds the audience of Christ's redemption of mankind. One of Walt's last sentences is that he has got a "light", which refers to his function as a symbol of hope in the darkness. In contrast to Jesus, Walt seeks to atone for his own sins, but he also manages to restore law and order in the neighborhood. In a figurative sense, both end up at a cross. Whereas Christ is crucified, Walt stretches out his arms, by which he forms a cross when he lies dead on the ground.

The Ambiguity of Belonging

> **INFO AT A GLANCE**
>
> **Cultural and social identity problems**
> - Thao is torn between his Hmong traditions and his wish to assimilate into American society.
> - All people around him emphasize Thao's female character traits and behavior. He searches for a clear male identity.
> - Having resisted the overall white flight, Walt lives alone amidst a Hmong dominated community in which he does not fit.
> - He recognizes that he has more in common with his Hmong neighbors than with his own family.
> - Walt is also "alienated from himself" (Ulmer 2017, p. 52).

Hmong as a people have no defined place in the world	Both Thao Vang Lor and Walt Kowalski have cultural and social identity problems. This is true for the teenager in a multiple sense, as the Hmong in general have no defined place in the world. In Asia they live scattered throughout Thailand, Laos, Vietnam and China. They understand themselves as a people with a common culture, language and religion. However, not in all of the above mentioned countries they are accepted as a minority. In Vietnam they were persecuted by the communists, so that they had to flee to the United States. This feeling of not knowing where one belongs to must be prevalent in the Lor family, in particular in Phong's generation.

Thao himself was born in the U.S. Legally, he has a clear status as a Hmong American. However, with respect to his cultural identity, he is torn between his family roots and the expectations of white American society. His grandmother and his mother are quite traditional, his absent father is described as "old school". Phong and his mother do not speak English. They never really tried to assimilate into American society but tried to uphold their culture in the foreign country.

Traditional Hmong family unwilling to assimilate

The teenager, however, has to find his place between Hmong tradition and the American culture. He went to school in the U.S., dresses according to young American dress codes (jeans, T-shirt) and speaks both languages. He definitely wants to assimilate more than his parents. It is remarkable that he secretly leaves the birth ceremony. Obviously, he does not take the obligatory presence in the old rituals for granted anymore. Nevertheless does he choose a Hmong girlfriend. At Walt's funeral, he wears his traditional Hmong clothes.

Thao is torn between Hmong and American cultures

Thao's unclear gender identity starts with his name. According to Ulmer (2017, p. 52), Thao is "usually a girl's name", but is also the title of a Thai nobleman or noblewoman. Additionally, Thao is teased with his feminine appearance which in part is a result of his not having started to grow a beard. The differences to his peers are striking. They rebel against their fathers' world and organize themselves in gangs. Spider is tattooed, his beard shows his masculinity. He and the other gangbangers live according to their own rules. In contrast to them, Thao is bossed around by his sister Sue and does work considered to be women's duties like washing the dishes and gardening. Even his grandmother Phong believes that he will never become "the man in the house."

Thao – a girl's name and a title

Differences to his peers

Walt keeps on calling him "pussy", signaling that he misses in Thao the masculine character trait of standing up to something. Replying to Thao's remark that he is willing to take any of Walt's racist insults, the old man tells him:

"Pussy" kid

> "Yeah, course you'll take it, because you have no teeth, you have no balls, kid." (55:09)

Male identity: a girlfriend, a car and a job

The veteran helps him in becoming a real man. He teaches him to talk like a man and provides him with a job in construction, stereotypically a male-dominated field. The 16-year-old Hmong follows Walt's advice and begins to date Youa. Probably the most important lesson for Thao is to rely on himself. With the "muscle car", the Gran Torino, he is finally equipped with everything which makes up a complete male identity: a girlfriend, a car and a job. In the final scene in which he drives alongside Lake St. Clair, it is clearly shown that he has grown a beard.

Walt as the only white man in a Hmong neigborhood

Walt Kowalski, on the other side, suffers from a different ambiguity of belonging. With his skin color and cultural background he does not fit in with the new Hmong neighborhood. All whites have moved away to the richer residential districts, as is illustrated by Walt's two sons. In former times Walt felt at home in Highland Park when the area was inhabited by workers from the automobile factories. Lots of the lower middle-class people were from Poland, like Walt's former next-door neighbor Polarski. With him and other white people Walt shared the same values such as patriotism and the ideal of white predominance in U.S. society. Keeping up your house and your front lawn were unwritten laws to present a perfect façade of an American idyll.

Walt as an old timer in a fast-changing world

Walt feels like "the last survivor of an older generation of 'real Americans' with 'decent' conservative values" (Ulmer 2017, p.52). However, in reality he is an outdated model in a fast-changing world. Like his Gran Torino, he does not fit in with the present time anymore. No wonder he is unhappy, wants to be left alone and avoids any contact to his neighbors.

Torn between two families

Equally painful for him is the fact that he is alienated from his family. He does not appreciate that they moved away and prefer to drive a Toyota instead of an American car. Walt is deeply hurt that they have no time for him. He suffers from the inner distance that is between them but he has not been able or willing to bridge the gap between them. It is a crucial moment in the movie when he has to recognize that he has more "in common with these gooks" than with his "own spoilt-rotten family." He really appreciates the Hmong's sense of community, their respect for the old and their hanging on to their cultural traditions. Despite his racial prejudices he accepts the Hmong neighbors as his substitute family.

Additionally, Walt is "alienated from himself" (Ulmer 2017, p. 52). Against his personal beliefs and values he killed innocent people in the Korean War. He also failed in being a good father. Both facts make him feel guilty. He finally is at peace with himself, as he confesses to Father Janovich. He finds a way out of his personal crisis by sacrificing himself. Last but not least, Walt's relation to the Catholic faith remains unclear. He is rather distanced to the Catholic Church as an institution and went there only for his wife's sake. He strongly objects to go to confession. On the other hand, he develops a very close relationship with Father Janovich. Thus the ambiguity of belonging can be observed on various levels, determined by cultural and social, but also very personal factors.

Alienation from himself

Unclear relation to the Catholic faith

Analysis and Interpretation

Symbols and Motifs

INFO AT A GLANCE

The Gran Torino and the motif of life and death dominate the movie
- The Gran Torino fits to Walt Kowalski's personality as it expresses his masculinity.
- It is a necessary part in Thao's process of becoming a man.
- The vintage car bridges the gap between Walt and Thao. It is a symbol of the family connection between them.
- The mirror stands for Walt's moments of introspection.
- The lighter is a reminder of Walt's guilt.
- Life and death, the main motif of the movie, are juxtaposed. Death is present and foreshadowed throughout the movie by the two funerals, Walt's smoking, his coughing up blood and the final shootout.
- The movie plays with gender stereotypes.

Cars express people's personality

According to Leslie Rendall, the Curator of the Peterson Automotive Museum in Los Angeles, most men choose a car which expresses their personality (cf. his commentary in the short documentary "Manning the Wheel" on the DVD *Gran Torino*). This definitely applies to Walt Kowalski and explains the famous quote by the movie's director:

"Walt sort of is the Gran Torino"

> "The car is just a symbol for a part of Walt. Walt sort of is the Gran Torino." (Clint Eastwood, in: "Manning the Wheel", special feature on the DVD *Gran Torino*)

Close relation with the car

The Gran Torino and Walt himself are somehow relics of a former time. As he put the steering column in the car, he himself made it. His pride is best shown in the scene, when he is sitting on his porch after having polished the Gran Torino, saying: "Ain't she sweet!" The personal pronoun reveals an affectionate relationship with the car, as if it were a human being. On the other hand, the so-called "muscle car" perfectly matches his masculinity. With its enormous horsepower, the Gran Torino signals strength, allowing a sportive and showy driving-style. Its distinct sound corresponds to Walt's growls. Moreover, the car from the 1970s stands also for America's glorious industrial past and its values in which Walt still believes. Even its name reminds at least the older viewers of the grand days of U.S. entrepreneurship.

For Thao, the car also is an essential part of his male identity. For most male teenagers, owning a car is some kind of rite de passage:

> "I think every adolescent goes through that feeling of attaining freedom when you finally get your wheels, you know. And you can leave the nest and you can go out with your buddies. And then, more importantly, eventually pick up girls and take them away from their homes and on dates." (Bill Gerber, Producer of *Gran Torino*, in: "Manning the Wheel")

Importance of cars in the life of adolescents

Thao cannot believe his luck that his substitute father offers him the car for his date with Youa. However, Walt is convinced that he needs to take her out "more stylish[ly]" than going by bus. Generally, the vintage car brings Walt and Thao together. Ironically, first there is the initiation ritual of stealing the Gran Torino. Later in the movie, however, it bridges the gap between the two characters and their cultural backgrounds. Thao is seen polishing the car as Walt did before. It is not part of his compensational work or some sort of punishment, but rather a sign of Walt's confidence that he allows the Hmong teenager to deal with his most precious belonging, which foreshadows the fact that the car will finally go to Thao.

The Gran Torino brings Walt and Thao together

The car is handed over from "father" to "son" in three steps, thus establishing a family bond between the two. With Walt's offer to take the Gran Torino for dating Youa, the car is temporarily lent to Thao for the first time. It is very unlikely that Walt would have given it to Ashley in the same situation. Thus the symbolic act shows how close their relation has become which is the basis for Thao taking the Gran Torino after he has been freed by his sister in order to get to the gangbangers' house as fast as possible. Last but not least, it is quite natural that he inherits the car in the final scene. Walt has always hidden his treasure from his own family (cf. his pulling the canvas tarp over the car after Ashley has detected it). On account of the inner distance to his own relatives, they simply do not deserve the car. Even after Walt's death, the vintage car connects the two protagonists. While Thao as the new owner is driving alongside Lake St. Clair,

Handing over the car from "father" to "son"

Walt's symbolic presence after his death

Analysis and Interpretation

A means for assimilating

Walt is present by singing the title song "Gran Torino" in the background. The American car gives the Hmong teenager a new social status. It offers him not only a previously unknown mobility, but is also a further step in his acculturation. It is his chance to assimilate into American society.

Looking at himself in a mirror

At various stages of the movie Walt looks into a mirror which is a symbol of a new act of self-recognition or insight into his personality. The most prominent example is shown in the scene, when he finds out that he has more in common with his Hmong neighbors than with his own family. In a later scene he sees his own image just after he has been coughing up blood, knowing that he has to go to see his doctor (see picture below).

Walt's Zippo lighter is another important symbol in the movie. Although it has the traditional emblem of the U.S. Army 1st Cavalry Division, it is a token he carries around since 1951 and which constantly reminds him of his war crimes. When Walt sacrifices himself, there is a close-up of the lighter in his hand. On the one hand, this shows that he was shot innocently because he came unarmed. On the other hand, the lighter signals that he died to unload his burden. Finally, he is "at peace" with himself. Furthermore, the lighter has another positive metaphoric quality. Walt's remark that he has got a "light" leads to the interpretation that it also stands for the good in him. His death will bring light into the darkness and put an end to the gang's terrorizing the neighborhood.

Walt's lighter: token of his guilt

Walt's salvation is shown by his forming a cross with his arms stretched out on the ground after being executed by the Hmong gang. In contrast to Jesus who burdened himself with the sins of mankind, Walt Kowalski seeks to atone for his own sins. Closely connected to the ending, there is the motif of life and death which can be observed throughout the movie. Right from the beginning, life and death are juxtaposed. Dorothy Kowalski's funeral is contrasted with the Hmong birth ceremony next door. Walt's self-sacrifice allows Thao and Sue to live in peace.

The cross signals Walt's salvation

His death is foreshadowed on various levels. His coughing up blood seems to be a sign of terminal lung cancer. Apparently, he is about to be hospitalized. He continues with his excessive smoking although Mitch and Thao beg him to quit. Indeed, the cigarettes can be interpreted as "coffin nails", as his son phrases it. Additionally, there are his wartime experiences. Not only did he kill at least 13 people, but witnessed atrocities on both sides. His bad conscience leads to various conversations with Father Janovich whose main topic seems to be "life and death".

Father Janovich's favorite topic of life and death foreshadowing Walt's death

The frequent use of symbolic or real guns also belongs into this context. More than once Walt forms a gun with his hand in order to deter the Hmong gangbangers or the African American men. However, though owning two real weapons, he never fires a shot. On closer

Guns

analysis, this corresponds to the ending when he comes unarmed. The gangs, on the other hand, are ready to use their sub-machine guns, e.g. in the drive-by shooting and in Walt's execution.

Gender stereotypes

Another important motif is the allusion to gender stereotypes. For obvious reasons, this is closely connected to Thao. An impressive number of lines in the dialogues deal with the differences between men and women and the audience's expectations towards their behavior (cf. "Girls go to college, and the boys go to jail"). These phrases are linked to masculinity symbols like the men's magazine, guns and cars.

Cinematic Devices

Camera

> **INFO AT A GLANCE**
>
> **Point of view, dominance and intense emotions**
> - The camera supports the fact that the story is told through Walt's eyes.
> - Eastwood uses the high- and low-angle camera positions to indicate dominance or hierarchy; eye-level shots symbolize the equality of characters.
> - Close-ups are used in moments of intense emotions.
> - Long shots or establishing shots introduce a new setting.
> - In dramatic scenes the director chooses a hand-held camera.
> - Walt's death is filmed in slow motion.
> - Dissolves are used to underline the connection between two scenes or to indicate a change of location or the passing of time.

Camera perspective, angle, range and movement

Camera perspective, angle, range and movement are important cinematic means as they determine what we see in a movie and create certain effects. For obvious reasons, not every single remarkable shot can be discussed in this chapter. The following description rather aims at pointing out the most prominent examples. First of all it has to be mentioned that the camera perspective generally supports the fact that the story is told through Walt's eyes. Very often point-of-view shots are used to follow the events out of his perspective. A good example of this technique is the

Point-of-view shots

opening scene in which the widower observes the congregation of mourners coming into the church.

Another means creating a similar effect is to place the camera just behind the actor. This can be best observed in the scene when Walt finally challenges the Hmong gang. With him in the foreground, the audience looks at the gangbangers' house. However, this technique of identifying with the old man's point of view can also be used for the opposite purpose. When Walt makes his first racist remark ("How many swamp rats can you get in one room?"), the camera turns around him, creating a distance between the veteran and the viewer by leaving his point of view and showing him disdainfully spitting on the ground.

Camera behind the actor

Identification and distance

Camera angles are used in *Gran Torino* to indicate a dominance or hierarchy. Often they take advantage of the actors' height. In contrast to Clint Eastwood who is about 1,88m tall, Bee Vang (Thao) is only 1,65m (see picture below).

Taking advantage of the actors' different height

Analysis and Interpretation

Camera angles to indicate hierarchies	With shots from Thao's point of view, naturally the impression is created that he is looking up to his mentor or father figure. Their hierarchical relation is best exemplified in the scene when Walt and Thao talk about plans for the future. The teenager is kneeling in order to do some yard work, which minimizes his height. Walt, on the other hand, is standing in full size, thus looking down on the Hmong boy. In a series of over-the-shoulder shots and reverse shots from high-angle (Walt) and low-angle perspectives (Thao), the camera perfectly visualizes their "father" and "son" talk.
Dominance	In extreme situations of the movie, low-angle and high-angle camera positions indicate absolute dominance. This can be observed in the scene when Walt scares away the Hmong gangbangers after they tried to grab Thao. The low-angle camera moves up Walt's body before finally showing his fierce look and the rifle in his hand. Another example is the scene in which the veteran beats up Smokie. Worth mentioning is also the scene in which Walt towers over Thao who is locked up in the basement.
Increasing the threat	The same method applies to the presentation of Ahney Her (Sue) who is also quite small. The camera takes up her point of view when she is about to be harassed by the taller African American men, thus intensifying the threat.
Illusion of equality	On the other hand, the camera angle is also able to suggest the impression that two characters are on an equal level. This technique is used in Walt's and Sue's driving home after the incident just mentioned. With shots which deliberately miss out Walt's forehead and almost eye-level reverse shots from Sue's point of view, she seems to be almost the same size as Walt, visualizing her growing importance in teaching the veteran about Hmong history. The same trick can be observed in the dialogue between Thao and Tim Kennedy. Here Thao is
Eye-level shots to show Thao's new status	shown in eye-level shots, indicating his newly adapted manly status.
Camera range	As far as camera range is concerned, a classical device often applied in Hollywood movies is to use close-ups in moments of intense emotions. In *Gran Torino* these are

frequent, e.g. in the moment of Kor Khue's precise analysis of Walt's mind or Walt's confession of having killed an innocent teenager in the Korean War. Close shots can also focus on certain details which the audience might miss otherwise such as Walt's coughing up blood or the lighter in his hand after he has been shot down.

Close-ups and their functions

Long shots or establishing shots usually introduce a new setting. They are to be seen almost regularly at the beginning of the DVD chapters. Often these shots show a building from the outside such as the church in the opening scene, Walt's home, the Veteran's bar or the gangbangers' house. Another possibility of establishing a new situation is showing the arrival of certain people at a particular place. Among others, this is true for the scene in which Hmong guests approach the Lor house before the birth ceremony, Thao's confrontation with the Latino gang or the Hmong gangbangers' nightly attempt to take the teenager away by force.

Introducing a new setting

A common technique of visualizing dramatic tension is using a hand-held camera. With short cuts and a limited point of view, the unsteady pictures tend to create confusion. In *Gran Torino* this is applied in the fight between the Lor family and the Hmong gangbangers, the scene in which Thao gets his cheek burnt and in Walt's beating up Smokie. Last but not least, post-production editing techniques are apparently used in the movie to create special effects. Certainly, the filming of Walt's death in slow motion has to be mentioned in this context. By this means, the movie's anticlimax is highlighted.

Hand-held camera

Editing techniques

Slow motion

Additionally, the director of photography included dissolves in some scenes. The gradual overlapping of the last shot of a scene with the first one of the next scene underlines the connection between the two. Usually it also indicates a change of location or the passing of time. In *Gran Torino* this technique of superimposing a fade-out onto a fade-in is successfully applied in depicting Thao's transition from an insecure teenager to an adult male. There is also a sequence of dissolves when Thao works for the community under Walt's close scrutiny in

Dissolves in moments of special significance

Analysis and Interpretation

compensation for his attempt to steal the veteran's car. It is a period of a week which is summarized in about a minute of the movie. In this week the Hmong teenager rises to the tasks presented to him for the first time in his life. The odd jobs are quite strenuous, but his achievement makes him happy.

It is noteworthy that Eastwood uses the same editing device in the final scene as well. With Walt passing the car onto his "friend" Thao in his last will, the Hmong teenager is offered the last missing link to his male identity. The superimposed image of Thao standing in a corner of the law office to being the owner and driver of the Gran Torino conveys the strong impression that his ambiguity of belonging ends.

Music and Lighting

> **INFO AT A GLANCE**
>
> **Cultural and atmospheric indicators**
> - The melancholy title song "Gran Torino" picks up the main motifs of the movie such as the ambiguity of belonging, war scars, loneliness and disappointed dreams.
> - Drum sounds are frequent signals for dramatic tension. They indicate that Walt Kowalski is in his "war-mode".
> - The Latino and the Hmong gangs listen to music which reflects their own cultural background.
> - Low-key lighting corresponds to the melancholy atmosphere of the movie.
> - The bright daylight in the final scene supports the positive message of the movie.

Song expresses Walt's feelings

Loneliness, ambiguity of belonging and battle scars

Among the ten songs included in the soundtrack, the most prominent one is the melancholy ballad "Gran Torino" (Songwriters: Jamie Cullum, Clint Eastwood, Kyle Eastwood and Michael Stevens) which can also be listened to on the Internet (e.g. http://www.metrolyrics.com/gran-torino-lyrics-jamie-cullum.html#/ixzz4lIAkgs3X). It is full of Walt's bittersweet feelings. His dreams, encapsulated in the Gran Torino, have failed and turned out to be "bitter" experiences in life. A major motif of the song is loneliness ("A lonely rhythm / All night long / It beats"). Alienated from his own family and modern times, Walt suffers in a double sense, finding joy and orientation only in "old" streets which "shine with the things [he has] known." At the core of his unhappiness there are the "battle scars" from Korea. Having the feeling that he does not fit in anywhere anymore, he asks himself: "Do you belong / In your skin?"

As the ballad expresses a lot of Walt's interior problems, it is a clever idea to have it performed by Clint Eastwood himself. His voice connects him with Thao even after his death while the Hmong young man enjoys driving the Gran Torino and leaving his former life behind. Additionally, piano chords using motifs of the title song are blended over the sequence in which Thao shapes up the neighborhood. The same version is used after Walt's death when Thao, Sue and Father Janovich arrive at the scene of crime. All of them underline the general melancholy atmosphere of the movie *Gran Torino*.

First part performed by Clint Eastwood

Another predominant sound motif is the drum sound. Starting off with the title menue, low drum sounds are used as a reminder of the past. Set in the black-and-white context of the beginning, it is definitely a sound associated with Walt's military experiences in Korea. Later in the movie the sound indicates that the veteran is in his "war-mode" again. Thus it is to be heard in most of the dramatic scenes such as Walt's attempt to defend his Gran Torino against a burglar, his scaring away the Hmong gangbangers or in his confrontation with the African Americans. Of course, it is also present in the anticlimax when he finally challenges Smokie and his gang.

Military drum sounds as a reminder of the past

However, there are many more tracks included in the movie. Primarily they express a particular cultural background and preference of the presented characters. The Latinos, for example, listen to the Spanish rap song "Esto es Guerra", whereas the Hmong gangbangers play their respective music performed by Hmong or Asian music groups. The titles they listen to are tale-telling. Just before the confrontation with the Hmong, the Latino gangbangers listen to a song about war and violence. Smokie and Spider, on the other hand, obviously prefer songs like "We Don't F* Around" and

Music expresses cultural preferences

Tale-telling song titles

"All My Hmong Mutha F*kaz" (cf. soundtrack) which they listen to when they arrive at Thao's house in the darkness. In contrast to the harmonic melody of the title song, their music is rather dissonant, which is symbolic for the following fierce argument with the Lor family.

Low-key lighting as atmospheric marker

Not only the mentioned music is an atmospheric marker, but also lighting functions as a signal for the melancholy tone of the movie. To a remarkable extent Eastwood uses scenes with low-key lighting. This can be best exemplified by the scene in which Walt phones his son Mitch to inform him about his fatal disease. The scene is deliberately set in the evening. The dark lighting in Walt's room often expresses the desperate mood he is in, as for example in the scene after he hurt himself as a punishment for the escalation of violence.

Dramatic scenes in the darkness

Additionally, most of the dramatic scenes take place during the night. This is a cliché alluding to our fears in the dark. Limited visibility automatically creates suspense. This technique is perfectly accomplished in the scene in which Walt tries to stop Thao from stealing his Gran Torino. It seems as if Walt by chance touches a light bulb which, as a consequence, swings through the garage. However, this action, deliberately chosen by the director, just adds to the confusion of the unclear situation. However, with the great number of night scenes in mind it is more than remarkable that the movie ends with a scene in absolute bright daylight. This is definitely an indicator for the positive message of the film that there may be "Hope for [...] a Country" (Dargis 2008).

Positive ending in bright daylight

③ Fast Facts

Outline 1: Structure

Outline 2: Setting

Outline 3: Walt Kowalski

Outline 4: Thao Vang Lor

Outline 5: Multicultural Society

Outline 6: The Ambiguity of Belonging

Outline 7: Symbols and Motifs

Outline 8: Cinematic Devices

Outline 1: Structure (Arc of Suspense)

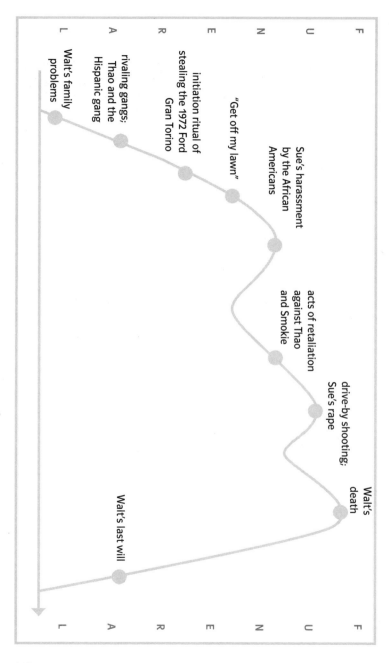

Outline 2: Setting

1. Highland Park

- until the 1960s a prestigious, white, middle-class neighborhood
- inhabited by car plant workers with the same cultural backround

⬇

- in 2008 a multicultural community
- in reality with over 90% African Americans
- in the movie a Hmong dominated, run-down neighborhood
- bad reputation for its crime rate
- Walt as the only white man left

White flight ➡

2. Rich residential districts

(cf. Mitch Kowalski's house)

Locations within Metro Detroit

3. Charlevoix St., Detroit

- symbolizes African-American "territory"
- Eastwood's intention: ghetto look and pictures of decay
- background: financial crisis 2008 which hit Motor City Detroit very hard

Fast Facts

Outline 3: Walt Kowalski

Walt is still haunted by his Korean War (1950–1953) memories: he killed at least 13 men, including one innocent teenager.

conservative values:

- hanging on to the past
- patriotism
- importance of family
- respect towards the old
- racial prejudices against Asians

manly behavior:

- hides his feelings
- solves his problems on his own
- is ready to use force
- owns a muscle car (the Gran Torino)

At the beginning of the movie Walt is shown as a grumpy old man alienated from his family. He does not belong to the changed neighborhood / modern America.

- He has to recognize that he has more in common with his Hmong neighbors than with his own family,
- develops a kinship towards Thao and Sue.

- He saves Thao and Sue,
- serves as a male role model for Thao.

Walt sacrifices himself in order to atone for his war crimes. Thus he wants to restore law and order in the neighborhood.

Outline 4: Thao Vang Lor

- easily persuaded by the Hmong gangbangers into stealing Walt's Gran Torino (initiation ritual)
- suffering from his resistance to join them (e.g. gets injured by them; drive-by shooting)
- finally ready to seek revenge for Sue's rape

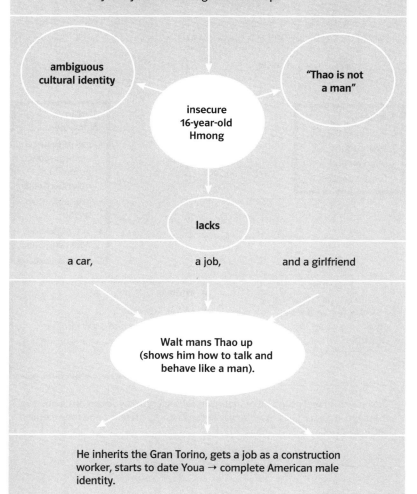

Fast Facts

Outline 5: Multicultural Society

Hmong
- first-generation immigrants (Phong and her daughter) keeping up their cultural traditions

gangbangers (Smokie, Spider)
- living according to their own rules
- protesting against their fathers' culture and terrorizing the neighborhood

Thao and Sue
- trying to assimilate, e.g. Sue dates Trey, a white teenager

Gang rivalries

Latinos
- live up to their own culture (e.g. music)
- have weapons

Ethnic groups live in parallel worlds
→ gloomy picture of a segregated society

African Americans
- live in their own run-down, ghetto-like neighborhood
- probably have no job
- aim at sexually harassing Sue

Exception: multicultural mix at Dr. Chu's (Asian doctor, Muslim assistant, patients of various ethnic groups)

Whites
- Walt Kowalski
- Mitch, Steve and their families
→ white flight to the rich residential districts of Detroit

Despite its critical portrayal of multicultural society, *Gran Torino* has a positive message. If a racist like Walt Kowalski can change, there is hope for American society as well.

Outline 6: The Ambiguity of Belonging

Hmong tradition
- educated by his "old-school" father to live according to Hmong values
- wears his traditional costume at Walt's funeral
- Hmong girlfriend

female traits
- female appearance
- bossed around by his sister
- does women's work (washing the dishes, gardening)
- does not meet the expectations of being the man in the house
- Walt calls him "pussy" for his passiveness.

American tradition
- usually follows young Americans' dress code (jeans, T-shirt)
- does not take part in the birth ceremony
- wants to assimilate

male traits
- finds a male role model in Walt
- learns how to talk like a man
- gets a job in a male-dominated field (construction)
- starts dating Youa
- finally inherits a "muscle car"

← Cultural belonging →

THAO

← Gender role →

- Highland Park used to be a white middle-class area.
- Walt is the only one who resisted white flight.

- feels like "the last survivor of an older generation of 'real Americans' with 'decent' conservative values" (Ulmer, p. 52).

- alienated from his own materialist family, in particular his grandchildren.

- critical distance to the Church as an institution, e.g. he does not go to confession.

← Neighborhood →

WALT

← Values →

← Family →

← Catholic Church →

- nowadays a Hmong dominated community (in reality the racial makeup of Highland Park is more than 90% African American).

- is attracted by the Hmong's upholding of their traditions.

- has to recognize that he has more in common with his Hmong neighbors than with his own family.

- develops a close relationship with Father Janovich.

Outline 7: Symbols and Motifs

The Gran Torino

- The "muscle car" corresponds to Walt Kowalski's personality as it expresses his masculinity.
- It is a symbol for Walt being an "outdated model" in a fast-changing world.
- It represents conservative American values.
- It is a necessary part in Thao's process of becoming a man.
- The vintage car bridges the gap between Walt and Thao. It is a symbol of the family connection between them.

Mirror

- symbol of Walt's introspection, e.g. when he finds out that he has more in common with the Hmongs than with his own family.

Lighter

- symbol of Walt's Korean War experiences
- constant reminder of his guilt

Gender stereotypes

- playing with the audience's conception of men and women

Cross

- lying on the ground with his arms spread out in the moment of death
- symbol of Walt's salvation

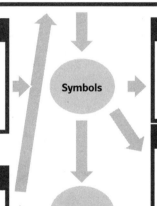

Life and Death

- The movie is framed by two funerals.
- Life and death are often juxtaposed, e.g. Dorothy Kowalski's funeral and the Hmong birth ceremony; Walt's self-sacrifice allows Thao and Sue to live in peace.
- Father Janovich's favorite topic is "life and death."
- Walt's excessive smoking and his coughing up blood foreshadow his own death.
- Walt killed at least 13 men in the Korean War, including an innocent teenager.
- The American Constitution warrants the right to bear arms.
- There is gang violence and a final shootout.

Outline 8: Cinematic Devices

Camera

Perspective
- Point-of-view-shots support the idea that the story is narrated through Walt's eyes; alternatively, the camera is placed behind the actors.

Angles
- Low- and high-angle camera positions create the illusion of a hierarchy, in particular between Walt and Thao.
- In extreme situations these are used to express absolute dominance, e.g. when Walt scares away the Hmong gangbangers.
- African Americans seem more threatening when filmed from below.
- Camera position, on the other hand, equalizes the difference in height between Walt and Sue in order to show their similar status.
- Eye-level shots on Thao in the interview with Tim Kennedy indicate his recently acquired manhood.

Range
- Close-ups in moments of emotional intensity, e.g. after Kor Khue's analysis of Walt's mind
- highlighting important details, e.g. the lighter
- long or establishing shots introducing new scenes or settings

Hand-held camera
- in moments of dramatic tension, usually with extreme short cuts

Music

The title song "Gran Torino" refers to main themes of the movie such as
- not to know where one belongs to
- loneliness
- bitter experiences in life
- shattered dreams

Drum sounds
- reminder of Walt's Korean War experiences
- used in scenes of violence or threats

Cultural markers
- Latinos listen to Spanish rap about war.
- Hmong gangbangers prefer Asian or English disharmonic music.

Lighting

- often low-key lighting to express melancholy or depression
- final scene (Thao driving along Jefferson Avenue / Lake Shore Drive) in bright daylight which corresponds to the positive message of *Gran Torino*

④ Model Tasks and Answers

1. Walt and Thao

2. Walt and his Family

3. Portrayal of the Hmong Community

4. Ambiguous Identities

5. Guilt and Redemption

6. Language

7. *Gran Torino* – A Portrait of Contemporary America?

8. *Gran Torino* and Tom Franklin's Novel *Crooked Letter, Crooked Letter*

1. Walt and Thao

Describe the relationship between Walt Kowalski and Thao Vang Lor.

Ignorance and racial prejudices

- Walt Kowalski and the Lor family seem to have lived next to each other for quite a while but there has been no contact between the two families as they belong to different cultures.
- Walt "is still living in the '50s", when the neighborhood was inhabited by white middle-class people, somehow connected to the automobile industry. Every time he sees the Hmong family's lawn, he is reminded of the good old times with his Polish neighbor Polarski.
- Since the Korean War (1950–1953) he has been racially prejudiced against all "gooks". For him, all Asians look alike.
- He does not belong in Highland Park anymore because the neighborhood is dominated by the Hmong. He is the only white man left; like his own children, all other whites have moved away.
- Alienated from his own family and modern times, he is a grumpy old man who wants to be left alone.
- At the beginning of the movie, the two families are not aware what is happening in the lives of each other. So Thao does not seem to know that Dorothy Kowalski has just died and that there is a funeral feast.
- In their first meeting, when Thao asks for jumper cables, Walt briskly slams the door in his face, uttering his usual racial slurs.

A failed initiation ritual

- Ironically, Thao's attempt to steal Walt's Gran Torino brings the two protagonists together. Walt wakes up in the middle of the night thinking that there is a thief in the garage, not recognizing it is Thao, who can escape.
- In an act of self-defense Walt scares away the Hmong gangbangers ("Get off my lawn"). However, for the Hmong community he is the savior to the neighborhood.
- Obviously, particularly the Lor family owes him a lot. They are ashamed that Thao tried to steal the car for which the teenager apologizes to Walt.

Turning-point

- On his birthday Walt observes Thao help a woman on the other side of the street with her spilled groceries. This breaks the ice in their relationship.
- Thanks to Sue's initiative, he joins in the Hmong barbecue. Although Thao

is a complete stranger, Walt starts criticizing him for his passiveness with regard to Youa.

Taking Thao under his wing

- The basis for their getting into touch is Walt's painful recognition that he has "got more in common with these gooks than with [his] own spoilt-rotten family."
- Thao wants to work off his guilt. In the week in which he does odd jobs for the community under Walt's close scrutiny, he starts developing into a man.
- Another important step in getting to know each other better is that they need mutual help. The Hmong teenager asks the old veteran for help with the faucets, whereas Walt cannot move a heavy freezer up from his basement.
- Thao begins to look up to Walt who becomes a male role model for him.
- Like father and son, they talk about Thao's future which does not look bright as he has neither money, a car, a job nor a girlfriend.
- Walt decides to "man him up".
- Together with his friend Martin they teach the teenager how to talk like a man.
- Walt vouches for him so that Thao gets a job in construction, a male-dominated field.
- Walt invites Thao, Sue, their mother and Youa to an American barbecue. His guests seem to be his substitute family. Quite remarkably, Walt lets Thao take his Gran Torino for his date with Youa.

Walt's guilt and sacrifice

- The old veteran recognizes that he is to be blamed for the drive-by shooting and Sue's rape. Despite Thao's explicit wish not to do anything in retaliation for the gangbangers' attack on him, Walt beats one of them up. He must have known that this would trigger a fierce reply.
- Walt tricks Thao into his basement and locks him up, telling him that he himself has blood on his hands (from Korea) and therefore wants Thao to stay away. He is going to confront the Hmong gang alone.
- He sacrifices himself so that Thao and Sue can live in peace.

Epilogue

- Even after his death Walt and Thao are linked together.
- In his last will Walt leaves the Gran Torino to his "friend" Thao Vang Lor. This completes Thao's male identity and offers him a means for further assimilation into American society.

- As Thao is driving alongside Lake St. Clair, Walt's (Clint Eastwood's) voice accompanies him with the song "Gran Torino".

Summing up, the movie tells the story of two characters who are influenced by each other and change due to their developing relationship. Walt unexpectedly turns from a grumpy old man and detached racist into a positive father figure for Thao. With the help of Walt, Thao grows from a teenager into a male adult.

2. Walt and his Family

Analyze Walt's relation to his family.

Opening scene at Dorothy's funeral

- The movie begins with Walt standing apart from his family which symbolically expresses the inner distance between them.
- The widower growls loudly when he witnesses his granddaughter is dressed indecently with a bare midriff and a belly piercing. Later she is seen using her smartphone during the service.
- Her brother mocks the Catholic tradition of kneeling down and making the sign of a cross.
- Walt's son Mitch obviously does not object to his children's behavior.
- Mitch and Steve criticize that their father is "still living in the '50s." They are fed up with the experience that every time they meet Walt seems to argue about something. Thus they stopped inviting him for Thanksgiving. Neither of them wants Walt to move into their house.
- The opening scene makes clear that the relationship between Walt and his family is rather distanced.

Materialistic interests versus conservative values

- One reason for their estrangement is a conflict of values.
- Walt's patriotism is not only shown by the flag on his porch but also in his choice of an American car. Of course, this is also due to his lifelong work at a Ford factory.
- Mitch, on the other hand, looks for his own profit in the globalized world. He cannot see any fault in selling Toyotas. He himself has a Toyota Land Cruiser.
- Mitch's and his wife Karen's primarily materialistic interests can also be concluded from the phone call in which Walt does not believe that Mitch only wants to know whether everything is fine. Significantly, the widower asks his son what he really wants, after Karen has gone through all of Dorothy's jewelry. He suspects some further request. It is a shame that he is right because it turns out that his son only asks for some season tickets Walt might organize for them.
- Later, when Walt possibly wants to tell him about his fatal disease, Mitch is busy with bills.
- In the final scene Mitch, Steve and their families are shocked that Walt has given all his possessions to the Catholic Church and Thao.
- Walt, on the other side, is rather "old school" in his values. Although he is critical towards the Catholic Church as an institution, he nevertheless

demands respect for the sacredness of the ritual. He has been taught in his youth to respect and to care for the old, which he now seems to expect from his family as well.
- For obvious reasons, he hides his treasure, the vintage car, from his family under a canvas.

Walt and Ashley

- Ashley is portrayed as cold-hearted. She does not seem to mourn about her grandmother's death at all. She is just bored as there is no connectivity for her cellphone in Walt's house.
- When Walt finds her having a smoke in the garage, she literally wishes him dead in order to get the Gran Torino ("What are you gonna do with it, when you, like, die?"). No wonder, her grandfather leaves her without a comment. However, his spitting out on the doorstep symbolically shows his contempt for her.
- Despite her incredible behavior she still believes that Walt will pass the car onto her after his death.

No communication

- There is no real communication between Walt, his granddaughter and his sons.
- Significantly, Steve does not get in touch with his father throughout the whole movie. He is only present at the two funerals.
- Obviously Walt is deeply hurt that his sons have no time for him. This can be concluded from his remark to Steve when he is about to get some chairs from the basement. Replying to his son's offer to do that for him, he says that he needs the chairs now, not next week.
- These experiences culminate in the scene with Walt sitting over his hospital admittance form calling Mitch. First of all, no one in Mitch's family wants to answer the call once they see that it is Walt. It remains unclear whether Walt would have told his son about his fatal disease, because their conversation comes to an abrupt end, as Mitch explains that he is busy.
- In general, Walt is not used bothering his sons with his own problems. Thus he does not tell Mitch about the nightly burglary either.

Complete estrangement

- That his sons are completely out of touch with their father is most obvious in Mitch's and Karen's visit on Walt's birthday. They treat him as if he were disabled, no longer able to live his ordinary life as before. They do not understand why Walt is appalled by their presents and kicks them out.

- All these factors indicate that Walt is completely alienated from his family.
- However in his confession to Father Janovich, he admits that he suffers from that inner distance.

3. Portrayal of the Hmong Community

1. Describe how the Hmong community is presented in the movie.
2. Despite the general appraisal of *Gran Torino*, the movie has also been criticized for confirming stereotypes. Discuss that with respect to the Hmong.

Hmong history

- *Gran Torino* is the first Hollywood movie which deals with the fate of the Hmong, a small, rather unknown ethnic minority in the U.S.
- As explained by Sue, the Hmong supported the Americans in the Vietnam War. After the communist takeover they were persecuted, so many of them fled to the U.S.
- The Lor family came to the U.S. after 1980.
- Hmong belong to the poorest ethnic groups in America. They are also troubled by a low level of education and gang violence.

First and second generation immigrants

- Phong and her daughter Vu represent the first generation of immigrants. They hang on to their cultural traditions and do not speak English. Particularly Phong is rather prejudiced against white America.
- Second-generation Hmong Americans show different levels of integration into American society. Sue seems to be most assimilated as she has a white boyfriend. However, this is obviously not true for the Hmong gangbangers who live according to their own rules.

"The girls go to college, and the boys go to jail"

- Sue seems to confirm the well-known fact that Hmong girls generally fit in better.
- She is very smart and often shows her intellectual superiority towards her peers.
- She has no difficulty in switching between Hmong culture and the American way of life.
- She bridges the gap between Walt and Thao.
- Thao is rather doubtful about which direction to take. Thus he is easily persuaded into stealing the Gran Torino. If the initiation ritual had not failed, he might have ended up in the Hmong gang and – finally – in jail.
- Smokie and Spider rebel against their fathers' culture and terrorize the neighborhood. Obviously, they have no job. Instead they hang around with their peers and cruise with their souped-up Honda.

- The main characters seem to correspond to stereotypes of Hmong Americans.
- An exception is the Hmong police officer who explains the circumstances of Walt's death to Thao and Sue.

Fatherless youngsters?

- Certainly there are Hmong male adults (cf. at the birth ceremony), but they seem to have lost their function of being male role models.
- Either they are physically absent (as in Thao's family) or they do not know the answers to the problems arising in their new surroundings.
- Thao's and Sue's father was really "old school" which means that he tried to raise his children according to Hmong traditions without preparing them for American life.
- The fathers of the gangbangers are absent, too. At least they do not do anything against the youngsters' crimes.

Poverty

- In contrast to Walt's neatly kept house, the Hmong homes seem to be run-down.
- Probably due to a lack of money, the houses are in a bad shape. Most things are in need of repair (cf. faucets, ceiling fan).

Confirming stereotypes?

- With respect to current issues of the Hmong community such as poverty, unemployment or gang violence, *Gran Torino* presents a realistic picture.
- Nobody worries about confirming positive stereotypes such as "Asian girls are supposed to be smart" (Walt).
- Even the claim that "girls go to college" and "the boys go to jail" is an accepted generalization since it corresponds to real life.
- However, real members of the Hmong community criticize that Hmong people are stereotypically portrayed as docile and passive so that they cannot solve their own problems and need support.
- This criticism has to be countered by the argument that *Gran Torino* is a drama with its own rules and not a documentary.
- The whole story is not about Asians and their more or less successful integration into American Society, but about Walt Kowalski who tries to come to terms with his past and atone for his guilt.
- It is in the logic of Clint Eastwood's movies that the plot centers on him, often with a violent shootout.
- Thus it is almost inevitable that Walt becomes the "hero to the neighborhood".

This includes his confronting the gangbangers alone at the end of the movie.
- Summing up, although stereotypes are confirmed in the portrayal of the Hmong community, Clint Eastwood also came up to the expectations of the audience.

4. Ambiguous Identities

Discuss whether and in which way Walt, Thao and Sue suffer from an ambiguity of belonging.

Walt

- The ambiguity of belonging describes the feeling of not fitting in with the changed conditions of life. Walt especially complains about the fact that he lives in a neighborhood dominated by Hmong Americans:
  - Highland Park used to be a white middle-class community.
  - Like Walt, most people were somehow connected to the automobile industry.
  - With his former next-door neighbor Polarski Walt shared the same values such as the importance of keeping up one's property.
  - Walt resisted white flight so now he is the only white man left in an all-Asian neighborhood.
- With his conservative values dating back to the 1950s, he does not fit in with modern American society. Like his vintage car, he seems to be an old timer in his attitudes with special respect to his
  - ideal of white predominance,
  - racial prejudices against minorities,
  - respect for the old,
  - family values,
  - exclusive preference of American cars.
- He is definitely torn between his own family and the Lor family next door:
  - He is completely alienated from his own "spoilt-rotten" family.
  - As a worker at Ford, he cannot understand that his Yuppie son sells Toyotas and has moved to a rich residential district.
  - He is appalled by their materialistic worldview.
  - Walt regrets the fact that there is no proper communication between him and his sons (cf. his confession to Father Janovich).
  - It is quite painful for him to recognize that he has "got more in common with the gooks" next door. Walt finds in the Lor family what he misses with his own relatives: a certain adherence to cultural traditions.
  - In the end he is successful in overcoming his ambiguity of belonging. He seems to opt for his Hmong neighbors instead of his own family which can be seen from his invitation to a barbecue, his self-sacrifice and his leaving the car to Thao.
- However, his relation to the Catholic Church remains unclear:
  - Though rather distanced to the formal rituals of the Catholic Church such as going to confession, he expects respect from his grandchildren at Dorothy's funeral.

- Despite his reluctance to go to church, he opens his heart to its representative Father Janovich.
- In his last will he leaves his house to the Catholic Church.
• On the whole, Walt Kowalski suffers from an ambiguity of belonging. His feeling of being an outsider with respect to his cultural background and his values has made him a grumpy old man, a fact which reflects his severe identity crisis.

Thao

- The Hmong teenager has difficulties in finding his cultural identity:
  - His personal dilemma is increased by the general question of the Hmong people's geopolitical place. In Asia, they are scattered over Thailand, Vietnam, Laos and China. Due to political persecution after the Vietnam War, thousands of them immigrated into the U.S.
  - Thao is torn between Hmong and American cultures.
  - His father was "really old school", educating him according to Hmong traditions but did not prepare him for the American way of life.
  - His docility might be due to his cultural roots.
  - With respect to clothing, he usually dresses like other American teenagers. However, at Walt's funeral he wears his traditional costume.
  - He generally accepts the cultural traditions of his ancestors, but leaves the birth ceremony secretly.
  - In contrast to Ashley and many American teenagers, he prefers reading and is not addicted to a smartphone (he probably does not have one).
  - He tries to integrate into American society by learning the English language but lacks means for further assimilation such as a car or a job.
  - With respect to his girlfriend, he sticks to his own kind and chooses Youa.
- Furthermore, he is unsure of his gender identity.
  - In contrast to his male peers, his appearance seems to be somewhat effeminate (no tattoos, no beard, wears sandals).
  - Latino and Hmong gangbangers question his masculinity.
  - He is bossed around by his sister.
  - His grandmother Phong is worried that he does not match the expectation of being the man in the house.
  - Due to his passive and docile behavior, Walt keeps on calling him "pussy".
- Thao definitely suffers from an ambiguity of belonging as he is mocked at and criticized by almost everyone. For this reason he is unsure about which direction to take. As a consequence, he is easy to push around.
- However, with Walt's support as a role model, Thao is manned up and is finally successful in finding his male identity essential elements of which are having a car, a job and a girlfriend.

Sue

- Sue does not seem to suffer from being torn between two different cultures.
- She easily bridges the gap between her Hmong traditions and the American way of life.
- For these reasons she is able to develop a close relationship with Walt.
- She is more assimilated than all other Hmong characters in the movie. She even has a white boyfriend.

5. Guilt and Redemption

Describe how the topic of "guilt and redemption" is dealt with in *Gran Torino*.

"Guilt and redemption" is one of the main themes of the movie, closely connected with the Catholic Church and Walt's lifelong attempt to come to terms with the "horrible things" he did in the Korean War. Additionally, Walt has to be blamed for triggering a violent reply from the Hmong gangbangers.

Twofold guilt

- For five decades the veteran has lived with his bad conscience about war atrocities he witnessed and participated in.
- Personally he feels guilty for killing at least 13 Korean men.
- What haunts him most, is his shooting of an innocent teenager who only wanted to surrender. Apparently, Walt was not ordered to do so.
- However, Clint Eastwood does not give many specific details about Walt's guilt until the very end.
- Walt is also responsible for the spiral of violence between the Lor family and the Hmong gangbangers.
- He prevents Thao from being taken by Smokie and Spider who later take revenge on the teenager by burning a cigarette into his cheek. Despite Thao's explicit wish not to do anything in retaliation, Walt brutally beats up Smokie. He must have known that this would provoke a fierce reply.
- Realizing that it was his fault, Walt is completely shattered after the drive-by shooting and Sue's rape.

Confessions

- The Catholic Church offers a clearly defined, institutionalized way of dealing with one's guilt. A sinner goes to confession and admits his deeds to a priest in order to unload his burden.
- This is what Father Janovich has promised Dorothy Kowalski to pursue for her husband Walt.
- The veteran, however, does not want to confess to an "over-educated, 27-year-old virgin" fresh out of the seminary.
- When the old white man finally turns up to make a confession, Father Janovich is shocked, expecting Walt to plan something in retaliation for Sue's rape.
- To his surprise, Walt confesses only lesser sins such as kissing a woman back in 1968 and not paying his taxes. He is, in particular, seriously troubled by the fact that he has been unable to establish a good relationship with his sons, accusing himself of being a bad father.

- What disturbs Father Janovich most, is the fact that Walt admits that he is "at peace" with himself.
- In a similar scene the veteran eventually confesses to Thao what he did in Korea.
- In this second informal confession Walt admits that there has not been a single day in his life that he did not think of his war crimes.

Redemption

- Even after 50 years Walt has not been able to find a way to atone for his guilt from the past.
- After Sue's return, he punishes himself by hurting his hands with which he beat up Smokie and triggered the spiral of violence.
- However, he does not feel this to be sufficient to atone for his past guilt.
- He decides to sacrifice himself.
- The fact that he is about to die from lung cancer plays only a minor role. Even without this diagnosis, he might nevertheless have in this way taken the opportunity to atone for his lifelong guilt.
- He dies in order to allow Thao and Sue to live in peace.
- He himself can die in peace as well.
- His self-sacrifice is well-planned. He confronts the gangbangers unarmed so that they will not have "a chance" (to escape jail), as he promised to Father Janovich the night before.
- He deliberately pulls out his lighter, the symbol of his guilt, to make the gangbangers think he is going to produce a gun.
- When he lies dead on the ground, the lighter is still in his open hand, indicating that he is about to let it go.
- The crane shot from above shows that in his death Walt has spread out his arms thus forming a cross, the symbol of Christ's salvation.
- The association with Jesus Christ is evident in *Gran Torino*. However, there is a decisive difference. Whereas Christ redeems mankind from their sins, Walt seeks his own personal redemption.

Summing up, the theme of "guilt and redemption" is present throughout the film, and is associated with various clear symbols (lighter, cross, medal). It is inherent in Walt's past.

6. Language

Describe the role of language in the movie.

Marker of the level of integration

- Two languages are spoken in the movie: English and Hmong.
- Hmong dialogues and comments are usually subtitled. Kor Khue's analysis of Walt's mind is translated.
- In particular the older Hmong such as Kor Khue or Phong, who represent the first generation of immigrants, do not speak English.
- Even Vu who must have been in her twenties when she arrived in the U.S.A. failed to learn the language.
- Despite their new home country they keep on speaking their native language. The Hmong language in this context functions as a marker for their level of integration or assimilation which is obviously very low.
- This means that they cannot communicate with the people outside their community. This goes along with prejudices against (white) American people.
- The difficult relation between Phong and Walt is the best example for that.
- Young Hmong like Thao and Sue, on the other hand, are better integrated and speak English.
- The Hmong gangbangers communicate in English, too. Though not at all integrated, their rude or even vulgar mode of expression is their way of setting a clear distance to their fathers' culture.

Walt's language reveals that he is a racist

- Despite his development in the course of the movie, Walt continues calling Thao and other Hmong "swamp rats", "zipperheads" or "gooks".
- This is the way he and the other American soldiers referred to their enemies in the Korean War. For Walt, all Asians look alike.
- He does not care about the Hmong names, although they correct him. Thus he calls Youa "YumYum" and Thao "Toad".
- Interestingly, he does not address the African Americans as "niggers" but calls them "spooks" only. Even in his joke at the Veteran's bar he talks about "a colored guy". That shows that Walt's racism is mainly limited to Asians of all kind.

Signaling masculinity

- Additionally, Walt's way of talking underlines his masculinity.
- His vulgar phrases and swearwords ("Come on, get the shit out of your head") are typically male.
- His commanding tone might be a consequence of his military career.
- The Hmong gangbangers use a register typical for male teenagers or young adults ("Yeah, man", "fuck" etc.).
- The same applies to the Latinos and the African American men.

Showing Thao's development

- The process of manning up someone is very difficult to show in a movie as it probably lasts for quite a while. *Gran Torino*, however, concentrates on two scenes: the episode at Martin's barbershop and the following conversation with the construction super.
- The change in Thao's language shows that he is in the process of taking on a male identity within his community.
- At first he obviously has no idea how to address an unknown male adult. His attempt to copy Walt's and Martin's exchange is rather feeble.
- He has to learn not only which words to use but also which topics to elaborate on.
- He is taught to follow stereotypical male conversation topics, such as women and cars.
- Surprisingly, in the next scene Thao is able to convince the super Tim Kennedy of his masculinity by fictitiously complaining about a garage owner who tried to cheat on him.

7. *Gran Torino* – A Portrait of Contemporary America?

Discuss to which extent the movie is a portrait of contemporary America (2008).

Decline of Motor City Detroit

- The movie was released in 2008, amidst the global financial crisis which hit the city hard.
- Two of the "Big Three" (General Motors and Chrysler) had serious financial problems, went into bankruptcy and had to be bailed out by the Obama Administration.
- Highland Park developed into an "industrial graveyard" (Dargis).
- *Gran Torino* shows some details of this decay especially with respect to the environment, e.g. when Sue and Trey bump into the African Americans.
- Although the scriptwriter Nick Schenk originally selected a Hmong community of Minneapolis, Minnesota, for the production and setting of the movie, Clint Eastwood thought Detroit much more suitable for a worker in the automobile industry.
- The high rate of unemployment in those years is implemented in *Gran Torino* by the gangs hanging around during the daytime.
- However, the movie is not about the crisis in American automobile industry. Its release in the middle of the economic downturn seems more or less accidental.

Multicultural society

- With focusing on the Hmong, a hitherto rather unknown ethnic minority in the U.S., *Gran Torino* does not fully take account of the proportions of ethnic minorities in contemporary multicultural society.
- Although 90% of Highland Park's population is of African American origin, they play a minor role only.
- However, official statistics confirm Walt's personal experience of being one of the last few white men in the neighborhood. According to the United States Census Bureau only 5.85% of the population in Highland Park is Caucasian (i.e. white).
- Corresponding to well-known developments in American society, the movie questions the ideal of white predominance. Members of certain ethnic minorities (especially of Asian origin) have risen to well-paid positions (cf. Doctor Chu).
- Additionally, *Gran Torino* shows a true picture of a racially segregated society.

- Whites left Walt's neighborhood and moved to richer residential districts (cf. Mitch).
- Hmong have formed an Asian-exclusive neighborhood.
- The African Americans speak of their "territory" on which Sue and Trey have infringed.
- Although people consider having racial prejudices is not politically correct, these preconceptions are widespread in the U.S.A. Walt is a typical example of white people not coming to terms with new developments in a multicultural society.

"Yes, we can"

- In his election campaign for presidency in 2008, Barack Obama used the memorable phrase "Yes, we can" in order to convince the people that he could introduce change.
- After eight years of conservative Republican government the majority of the American people longed for a new beginning.
- The beginning of Obama's presidency was met with high expectations.
- With the first African American president in office, the American people believed in a major improvement of race relations.
- In this context *Gran Torino* was regarded as one of the first movies fitting the new era.
- With a thoroughly prejudiced racist like Walt Kowalski developing into a friend of his Hmong neighbors, a lot of critics saw hope not only "for a racist, but maybe a country" (Dargis).
- Nobody could foresee that racial relations did not really improve. In fact, the number of African Americans being shot by white police officers drastically increased.
- Nevertheless, *Gran Torino* remains an outstanding, socially critical movie, which turns out to be ahead of its time.

As a conclusion one can argue that *Gran Torino* gives quite an accurate portrait of the U.S.A. at its time of release. However, in its positive, anti-racist message it offers a vision still waiting to come true.

8. *Gran Torino* and Tom Franklin's Novel *Crooked Letter, Crooked Letter*

Compare Walt Kowalski and Larry Ott, one of the protagonists in Tom Franklin's crime novel.

Mechanics

Both men have similar jobs.
- Walt worked at Ford.
- Larry Ott owns a garage in which he repairs the cars of by-passers.

Lonesome and embittered men

Both Walt Kowalski and Larry Ott live alone. They are presented as loners who don't rely on other people.
- Walt's wife Dorothy has just died.
- His social contacts are restricted to war buddies he meets at a bar once in a while.
- He celebrates his birthday alone on his porch.
- He is definitely embittered by the social developments in his neighborhood and disappointed about the disrespect of his sons and grandchildren.
- Larry Ott, on the other side, is shunned by the inhabitants of Amos, the small Mississippian town he lives in. They blame him for the disappearing of Cindy Walker twenty years before.
- Except for Silas Jones in his youth and the rather dubious relationship to Wallace Stringfellow, he has not had any friends in his life.

Cross-cultural friendships

Both protagonists develop an unusual cross-cultural friendship at some stage in their lives.
- The Korean veteran takes the 16-year-old Hmong teenager under his wing.
- He becomes a role model for Thao who really appreciates his help in manning him up.
- Despite Walt's racial prejudices, a close relationship develops between them.
- As a young boy, white Larry Ott befriends the African American Silas Jones, not knowing that he is his half-brother.
- Given the racism in rural Mississippi in the late 1970s, it is no surprise that in public (e.g. in school) Larry and Silas do not hang around with each other. However, they meet in secret outside of school.

- As they grow older, they get more distanced. Silas Jones leaves Amos. When he returns years later, he avoids contact with Larry who still seems to regard Silas as a friend when he is shot down (cf. his phone calls).

Suffering from feelings of guilt

Walt and Larry suffer from a strong sense of guilt due to some event(s) in the past.
- Walt has not come to terms with his Korean War experiences (1950–1953).
- He killed at least 13 people, witnessed and took part in various atrocities.
- What haunts him most, is the fact that he shot an innocent teenager.
- Only by his self-sacrifice at the end of the movie is Walt portrayed as redeemed from his guilt.
- Larry Ott is innocent, but people believe he raped and murdered Cindy Walker on a date with him back in 1982, as he was the last person to be seen with her. Presumably she was killed by her stepfather Cecil after she had secretly met Silas Jones who then was her boyfriend.
- Although there was no proof for Larry's guilt, people have shied away from him ever since. No one would ever stop at his garage.
- When Tina Rutherford disappears, he is the first to be suspected.
- Finally, Silas Jones's telling the truth clears him off all allegations.

Ambiguity of belonging

Both protagonists suffer from some ambiguity of belonging.
- Walt Kowalski is like an old timer in a fast-changing world. With respect to his values, he is still living in the 1950s.
- He is the only white man left in Highland Park, now a Hmong neighborhood.
- He is torn between his own family and his Hmong neighbors. It is painful for him to recognize that he has "got more in common with these gooks" than with his own relatives.
- Larry Ott has difficulties in finding his male identity.
- His attempts to gain acceptance by his peer group fail (e.g. jumping of the swing, yelling "Monkey Lips" to an African American girl).
- While the other boys play football, he prefers reading (in particular horror novels) and stays apart from the others.
- Compared to his male classmates, he is very shy. His date with Cindy Walker is mocked at by Ken and David who even want to spoil it.
- Like Walt, he is an outsider, not only at school. Due to the rumors about his killing the disappeared girl twenty years ago, he does not belong to Amos's community.

Difficult father-and-son relations

Walt and Larry have different and difficult father-and-son relations: Walt as a father, Larry as a son.
- Walt Kowalski is completely alienated from his two yuppie sons, who have moved to some rich residential district.
- While Walt is loyal to Ford, his son Mitch drives a Toyota.
- He is appalled by his sons' and their families' materialist worldview.
- They have almost no contact at all. When they are together, arguments are inevitable.
- As indicated in Walt's confession, he suffers from the fact that he did not find a way how to get closer to his sons.
- Larry Ott, on the other side, misses his distanced father.
- Carl Ott considers his son unsuitable for a career as a mechanic and does not take him to his garage (except for rare occasions).
- Carl Ott lets the two boys fight over his rifle.
- Larry's alleged crime estranges him from his father even more.

Bibliography

Analysis and Reviews

Dargis, Manhohla: Hope for a Racist, and Maybe a Country. New York Times, 11 December 2008; http://nytimes.com/2008/12/12/movies/12tori.html

Ebert, Roger: *Gran Torino*: "Get off my lawn"; https://2engom.wikispaces.com/file/view/%27Gran+Torino%27+Tasks+Booklet.pdf

Jalao, Ly Chong: Looking Gran Torino in the Eye: A Review. Journal of Southeast Asian American Education and Advancement Vol. 5 (2010); http://docs.lib.purdue.edu/cgi/viewcontent.cgi?article=1016&context=jsaaea

Ulmer, Friderike: Gran Torino. Lehrerhandbuch: Unterrichtsvorschläge und Kopiervorlagen. Stuttgart: Ernst Klett Sprachen, 2017. (Film im Englischunterricht.)

Machuco, Antonio: Violence and Truth in Clint Eastwood's *Gran Torino*; Anthropoetics XVI, No. 2 (Spring 2011); http://anthropoetics.ucla.edu/ap1602/1602machuco/

Links

http://www.materialserver.filmwerk.de/arbeitshilfen/AH_GranTorino_A4.pdf

http://www.racismreview.com/blog/2009/01/17/gran-torino-white-masculinity-racism/

http://kirstiendavis.weebly.com/gran-torino-film-analysis.html

https://sites.google.com/site/smartallect/analysis-of-gran-torino

http://www.kinofenster.de/download/gran-torino-pdf/

http://www.stern.de/kultur/film/-gran-torino--der-gute-rassist-3434260.html

https://prezi.com/rs7elhhiudtx/gran-torino

http://de.slideshare.net/WillDeAth/gran-torino-film-opening-analysis

https://bu.digication.com/wr100_section_1_north_end_caleigh_obrien/Artifact_9_Essay_2_Analysis_of_Gran_Torino_Through

http://www.beyondthescreen.com/sites/default/files/study_guide/Study_Guide_Gran_Torino.pdf

https://chadwickfilm.wordpress.com/2010/01/31/what-messages-does-gran-torino-convey/

http://www.masculinity-movies.com/movie-database/gran-torino

http://www.ethicsdaily.com/gran-torino-cms-13602-printer

http://lesmurdie-wa.libguides.com/english11/grantorino/analysis

http://reginatekulve.blogspot.de/2012/06/gran-torino-analysis-reflection-on.html

Hmong culture and history
https://en.wikipedia.org/wiki/Hmong_Americans
https://www.youtube.com/watch?v=cy_yHyq-ZxU
  (Next door=Hmong documentary, part 1)
https://www.youtube.com/watch?v=xC2zoxES45U
  (Next door=Hmong documentary, part 2)

Script and movie locations
http://www.imsdb.com/scripts/Gran-Torino.html
http://movie-locations.com/movies/g/GranTorino.html

Interview with Clint Eastwood on *Gran Torino*

https://www.youtube.com/watch?v=jXriv3tzXpw

Background Information on Clint Eastwood and his Movies

Cornell, Drucilla: Clint Eastwood and Issues of American Masculinity. New York: Fordham University Press, 2009.

Girgus, Sam B.: Clint Eastwood's America. Cambridge: Polity, 2014.

Hughes, Howard: Aim for the Heart. The Films of Clint Eastwood. New York: I. B. Tauris, 2009.

Schickel, Richard: Clint Eastwood: Ich bin nur ein Typ, der Filme macht. Eine Retrospektive. Hamburg: Edel, 2010.

Teaching Film

Donaghy, Kieran: Film in Action. Teaching Language Using Moving Images. Peaslake (Surrey): Delta Publishing, 2015.

Ryan, Michael / Lenos, Melissa: An Introduction to Film Analysis. Technique and Meaning in Narrative Film. Lonson/Oxford: Bloomsbury Publishing, 2012.

Index

A
Ashley 5, 16–18, 46, 49, 85, 87–89, 97, 124, 130
anticlimax 29, 42, 45, 48, 50, 103, 105

B
birthday (Walt's) 8, 29–31, 50, 58f, 87, 120, 124, 138

C
close-ups / close shots 21, 31, 39, 41, 44, 46, 100, 102f, 117

D
drive-by shooting 40, 50, 78f, 100, 110, 113, 121
drum sounds 23, 25, 28, 40, 45, 104f, 117
dissolves 34, 46, 100, 103

E
eye-level shots 100, 102, 117

F
father figure 102, 122
father-and-son relationship 86, 89, 121, 140
foreshadowing 8, 22, 29, 41, 50, 99, 116
funeral 5f, 15, 42f, 46, 49f, 55, 58, 70, 74, 89, 93, 99, 115f, 123, 129f

H
hand-held camera 23, 25, 39f, 100, 103, 117
high-angle shots 15, 20, 37, 45, 102, 117
Hmong traditions 20, 62, 68, 92, 127, 130f
horoscope 8, 29, 50, 59, 75, 91

I
initiation ritual 6f, 10, 21f, 37, 50, 62, 65, 83, 97, 110, 113, 120, 126
introspection 31, 75, 96, 116

K
Kennedy, Tim (construction super) 38, 66, 73, 84, 102, 117, 135

Korean War 5, 7, 17, 21, 23, 45, 50, 52, 74, 77, 89-91, 95, 103, 112, 116, 120, 132, 134
Kor Khue 31, 69, 103, 117, 134

L
low-angle shots 22, 25, 27, 34, 36, 40, 100, 102

M
Martin (Italian barber) 11, 26f, 33, 38, 43, 56, 66, 74, 82f, 121
masculinity 80ff, 93, 96, 100, 116, 130, 135
Mitch 7, 19, 24, 30, 33, 35f, 46, 49, 54, 56, 58, 85–87, 106, 114, 123f, 140
mirror 9, 31, 34, 60, 74, 96, 98, 116

P
prejudices 15, 20, 31, 49, 51, 54, 56f, 62, 68f, 73–75, 95, 112, 120, 129, 134, 137f
point-of-view shots 107, 117

R
racism 18, 74f, 82, 134, 138
retaliation 11, 26, 39, 41, 43, 50, 59, 62, 69, 71, 91, 110, 121, 132
revenge 39, 41f, 67, 71, 79, 91, 113, 132

S
self-recognition 9, 27, 96
slow motion 45, 100, 103
spiral of violence 41, 60, 69, 79, 91, 132f
Steve 15, 17, 85, 114, 123f

T
title song 15, 36, 45, 98, 104–106, 117, 122
turning-point 23, 31, 60, 120

W
white flight 52, 73, 92, 111, 114f, 129

Y
Youa 9, 11, 32, 40, 60, 67, 80, 84, 94, 97, 113, 115, 121, 130, 134

Z
Zippo lighter 45, 96, 99, 103, 116f, 133

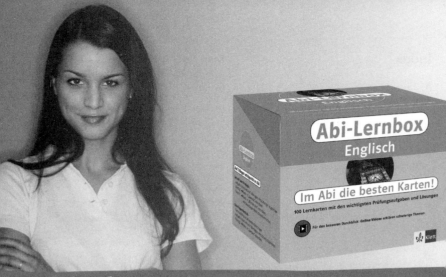

Die besten Karten im Abi

100 Lernkarten für das Abitur - mit den wichtigsten Fragen, die jeder beherrschen muss

Mit ausführlichem Hintergrundwissen auf der aufklappbaren Innenseite.

Mit Fächerunterteilung „Gewusst" und „Wiederholen" zur systematischen Prüfungsvorbereitung.

Inhalt: landeskundliche Informationen über GB und die USA, Grammatik, Vokabeln, Schreibkompetenz, Literatur verstehen und interpretieren.

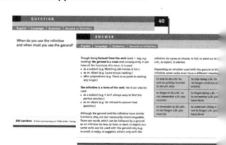

 Extra: Online-Videos erklären schwierige Themen!

Abi-Lernbox Englisch
100 Lernkarten mit den wichtigsten Aufgaben und Lösungen
ISBN 978-3-12-949327-4 | 19,99 Euro

Im Buchhandel erhältlich. Weitere Informationen unter **www.klett-lerntrainin**